Introducing the Bible

Introducing the Bible
An Active Learning Approach

Adam Porter
Illinois College

PEARSON

Prentice
Hall

Upper Saddle River, New Jersey 07458

Library of Congress Cataloging-in-Publication Data

Porter, Adam L.
    Introducing the Bible : an active learning approach / Adam L. Porter.
        p. cm.
    Includes bibliographical references.
    ISBN 0-13-177777-7
    1. Bible--Introductions. I. Title.

    BS475.3.P67 2004
    220.6'1--dc22

                                            2004005985

Editorial Director: Charlyce Jones-Owen
Senior Acquisitions Editor: Ross Miller
Assistant Editor: Wendy Yurash
Editorial Assistant: Carla Worner
Director of Marketing: Beth Mejia
Marketing Assistant: Kimberly Daum
Production Liaison: Marianne Peters-Riordan
Manufacturing Buyer: Christina Helder
Cover Design: Bruce Kenselaar
Composition/Full Service Project Manager: Jessica Balch, Pine Tree Composition, Inc.
Printer/Binder: Phoenix Book Tech

Pearson Education LTD., London
Pearson Education Singapore, Pte. Ltd
Pearson Education Canada, Ltd
Pearson Education—Japan
Pearson Education Australia PTY, Limited

Pearson Education North Asia Ltd
Pearson Educación de Mexico, S.A. de C.V.
Pearson Education Malaysia, Pte. Ltd
Pearson Education, Upper Saddle River,
    New Jersey

10 9 8 7 6 5 4
ISBN 0-13-177777-7

Contents

Preface

To the Instructor

Many schools require an Introduction to the Bible class because the Bible is one of the cornerstones of Western civilization. To appreciate Western art, literature, or civilization more generally, one needs to have some familiarity with the Bible. This need is important today, since many students know little about the Bible. Additionally, students, like the general population, are unfamiliar with critical Biblical scholarship. This textbook focuses on the latter issue, since carefully reading the Bible addresses the former.

This textbook is non-traditional. Most textbooks present facts and figures, summarize the Biblical text, and present scholarly ideas as "fact." Some seem to be glorified *Cliffs Notes* to the Bible. Students, pressed for time, often read the textbook more carefully than the Bible. My goal is to encourage students to read the Bible carefully and closely. I want students to analyze the text and reflect on it, to feel the thrill of discovering something new and interesting, rather than passively accepting the voice of an "authority." Since they practice the techniques used by scholars, they understand why scholars have the theories they do and can critique them.

Hence, students gain two things from this textbook: Biblical literacy and transferable skills. The former includes understanding major themes in the Bible, familiarity with major biblical characters, and knowledge of Biblical scholarship. The latter includes learning how to read carefully, to analyze texts, and to create persuasive arguments. These skills are the basis for all scholarship and students have the opportunity to practice them repeatedly going through this book.

To the Student

Students often find the Bible a morass of unpronounceable names, odd practices, and dull genealogies. This is understandable. I won't pretend that the Bible is easy to read or understand. (If it were, we'd need a lot fewer Bible scholars!) My goal is to lead you through the Bible, showing you how to read it carefully, as Biblical scholars do, and not be bored.

But while I can lead you, like the proverbial horse to water, I cannot make you drink. You must take responsibility to read the Bible carefully in order to answer the questions posed here. Many of these are rather straightforward, but will lead to more complex, analytical questions, marked with an asterisk.

Frequently, the analytical questions are ones that have puzzled readers and scholars. They are difficult questions to answer and different readers have offered more than one answer. Don't be discouraged if you cannot think of an answer or if your solution is different from your colleagues': this happens all the time to scholars! Think creatively and consider different possible explanations for the data you have collected and try to decide which you find most persuasive.

You may want to do additional reading on various topics. To help you with this, I have included a For Further Reading section at the end of each chapter. All further readings are from the *Anchor Bible Dictionary,* abbreviated *ABD.* There are two reasons for directing you to *ABD.* First, the dictionary can be found in almost every college library and many public libraries as well, so locating these references should be easy. Second, each article in the dictionary has a lengthy bibliography, so you can find additional materials easily.

Since the Bible *is* difficult reading, plan your time accordingly. It will take you longer to read Genesis than Tom Clancy or John Grisham. It will be harder to read, so find a quiet place with few distractions. Read with a pen (or pencil) in hand to underline material you find interesting or puzzling. Jot notes in the margins. And enjoy the exploration.

Acknowledgments

This textbook emerged from teaching a one semester "Introduction to the Bible" class at Illinois College. I have received much feedback from my students and their comments and questions have guided much of the writing in this text.

My two student assistants, Sara Brown and Rebecca Cobb, have helped me in innumerable ways, large and small. Evan Coonrod produced the maps.

My colleagues in the Department of Philosophy and Religion have encouraged me and supported my efforts, including "test-driving" the text in their classes. I am also indebted to my teachers and colleagues at Duke University, including Eric Meyers, Jack Levinson, Bart Ehrman, E. P. Sanders, Mark Chancy, and many others.

I appreciate my editor at Prentice Hall, Ross Miller, who has answered my questions and helped me see this project through to completion. The project manager at Pine Tree Composition, Jessica Balch, caught huge numbers of typos and other problems. Her patience and helpfulness have been unflagging.

Most importantly, my sons, Jonah and Isaiah, have kept me from living my entire life in the office and library. They have forced me to slow down and admire the wonder of bugs and butterflies, snails and slugs, lizards, and playing games. This is the world that really matters. This book is dedicated to them.

Adam Porter

PART ONE

Torah

Genesis, Exodus, Leviticus, Numbers, Deuteronomy

CHAPTER 1

Overview

What is the Bible? For Christians, it is the Old Testament and the New Testament. For Jews it is the Tanakh. Different Christians include different books in the Old Testament: the books included in the Apocrypha by Protestants are part of the Old Testament for Catholic and Orthodox Christians. Jews, Protestants, and Catholics all arrange the books in the Hebrew Bible differently.

This flexibility suggests that calling the Bible "the Good Book" is somewhat misleading. It is more properly viewed as an anthology, a collection of texts, which contains materials from approximately a thousand year period, written in Hebrew and Aramaic (for the Hebrew Bible) and in Greek (for the New Testament and Apocrypha).

We will work our way through the Hebrew Bible following neither Jewish nor Christian canons. Rather, in Part One, we will study Torah, the first five books of the Bible. In Part Two, we will examine books with historical narratives (Joshua, Judges, Samuel, Kings, Chronicles, Ezra and Nehemiah). And in Part Three, we will look at examples of everything else (Prophetic materials, Wisdom Literature, Psalms, short stories, and Apocalyptic).

In academic circles, the first five books of the Bible are often called the Pentateuch (from the Greek words for "Five Books"). Jewish tradition refers to these books

---

Alternative Terminology

Throughout this textbook, I will use the abbreviations BCE (Before the Common Era) and CE (Common Era) rather than the traditional BC and AD.

Many scholars prefer these abbreviations because they are inclusive and are not tied to Christian theology. Different religions use different dating schemes: Jews traditionally date the years from the day of creation, October 7, 3761 BCE; Muslims date years beginning with Mohammad's flight from Mecca in 622 CE. Thus, rather than privilege one tradition over another, scholars use the more generic BCE and CE.

I will use the term *Hebrew Bible* rather than *Old Testament* or *Tanakh* for the same reason: it is more inclusive and avoids sectarian overtones.

as Torah, sometimes translated "law" but perhaps more accurately rendered as "instruction." Although all five books are anonymous, as are many of the books in the Hebrew Bible, Jews and Christians traditionally attribute authorship of the Pentateuch to Moses, implying that they were written somewhat after 1250 BCE (the usual date for the Exodus out of Egypt). Most critical scholars doubt this attribution and also the date; we will consider why as we study the Pentateuch.

Whoever wrote it, the Pentateuch is the oldest portion of the Bible to be recognized as canon or scripture. By around 450 BCE, the five books had been collected and were used by Jews in public worship (see Neh 8:1–8). Because they are the oldest and most important part of the Hebrew Bible, they have been more closely studied in both religious and secular contexts than other parts of the Hebrew Bible.

Both Jews and Christians see the five books of Moses as the most important part of the Hebrew Bible, although for different reasons. Jews see Torah as directing people on how to live life in accord with God's instructions. Hence, the need to study Torah diligently, to understand it, and to observe it. Christians (largely because of Paul's emphasis on Torah) see the Pentateuch as documenting God's promises to humanity, which were fulfilled in Christ.

Much attention has been given to the question of authorship and literary composition of the Pentateuch. We will examine these questions using techniques developed by biblical scholars.

But before we turn to the Bible, we need to appreciate its setting among other Ancient Near Eastern cultures. To do this, we will read parts of the Eneuma Elis, a creation story from Mesopotamia. We will look for echoes of the Eneuma Elis in Biblical texts. One thing will quickly become evident: our modern concepts of who God is, what God does, and God's personality differ significantly from those of the ancients.

CHAPTER 2

Creation in the Ancient Near East

Read *Eneuma Elis* (appendix, pp. 287–295); Hab 3:8–15; Ps 74: 12–17; 89:5–13; 104:1–13, 24–26.

In this chapter we will:

- Read a famous creation story from the Ancient Near East, the *Eneuma Elis*
- See that the familiar creation story of Genesis 1 ("God said let there be light and there was light. . . .") is not the only description of creation in the Bible
- Think about the connections between the Ancient Near Eastern text and the Biblical narratives

Before you do this chapter, ask your roommate, a friend, or someone else the following questions:

1. How does the Bible say God created the world? What was there *before* creation?

2. How does the Bible describe God? What does God look like? How does God act?

Most modern people think of God in terms similar to those of Jonah: "I knew that you are a gracious God and merciful, slow to anger, and abounding in steadfast love, and ready to relent from punishing" (Jonah 4:2). These attributes are applied to God in many places in the Hebrew Bible (Exod 34:6, Neh 9:17, Ps 86:15, Ps 108:8, etc.).

But in addition to these familiar descriptions of God, the Bible offers other descriptions. In this chapter, we will explore some other descriptions of God. We will also see how they relate to the descriptions of divine beings found in other Ancient Near Eastern literatures.

Read the *Eneuma Elis* (Appendix, page 287).

Tiamat & Her Allies

A. In Greek mythology, Zeus is a storm god, Apollo is the sun god, Ares is the war god, and Aphrodite is the love goddess. In Mesopotamian mythology, what sort of goddess is Tiamat?

B. What is Tiamat's relationship to the other gods? (see Tablet I)

C. Who are Tiamat's allies and/or weapons? (see Tablet III)

Marduk & His Allies

D. In Mesopotamian mythology, what sort of god is Marduk?

E. How is his physical appearance described? (see Tablet IV)

F. How does he create things or cause them to come into existence? (see Tablet IV)

G. What is his relation to other deities? (see Tablet III)

H. When he goes out to battle, what are his weapons? (see Tablet IV)

I. How does he slay Tiamat? (see Tablet IV)

J. What does he do with her body? (see Tablet IV)

K. Why is humanity created and how? (see Tablet VI)

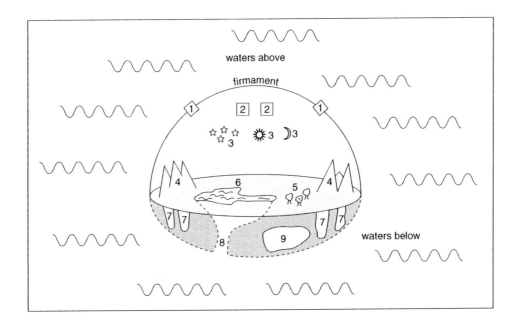

Figure 2–1. One difficulty in understanding creation stories from the ancients is that their *cosmology* (way of understanding the universe) was significantly different from ours. We think of the world as a spinning globe, one of nine planets circling the sun. They thought of the world as a bubble of air and land, surrounded by primordial, chaotic waters. This sketch offers one possible way of illustrating the Ancient Near Eastern cosmology.

Key to numbered items:

1. Windows of heaven (Gen 7:11)
2. Storehouses of hail and snow (Job 38:22)
3. Sun, moon, stars (Gen 1:14)
4. Mountains
5. Dry land (Gen 1:9)
6. Collected waters (Gen 1:9)
7. Pillars of the earth (1 Sam 2:8, Ps 75:3)
8. Fountains of the deep (Gen 7:11)
9. Sheol (Gen 37:35, Num 16:30, Job 17:13–16)

Now read the following passages from the Bible and answer the questions.

Habakkuk 3:8–15

A. What was God's mode of transport?

B. Who (or what) opposed God?

Biblical Citations

Scholars use a compact set of abbreviations to cite passages from the Bible. The three basic rules are:[1]

1. Books of the Bible cited without chapter or chapter and verse should be spelled out in the main text.
2. Books of the Bible cited with chapter or chapter and verse should be abbreviated, unless they come at the beginning of the sentence.
3. All occurrences of biblical books in parentheses and footnotes should be abbreviated.

Right: The passage in 1 Cor 5 is often considered crucial.

The passage, 1 Cor 5:6, is often considered crucial.

First Corinthians 5:6 is a crucial text.

"Do you not know that a little yeast leavens the whole batch of dough?" (1 Cor 5:6).

Wrong: 1 Cor 5:6 is a crucial text.

1 Corinthians 5:6 is a crucial text.

Verses may be subdivided by using a and b to indicate the first and second part of verses. Hence, Gen 2:4a refers to the first half of verse four of the second chapter of Genesis.

The standard abbreviations for books of the Bible are these:

Books of the Hebrew Bible

Gen	Genesis	Song	Song of Songs or Song of Solomon
Exod	Exodus	(or Cant)	(or Canticles)
Lev	Leviticus	Isa	Isaiah
Num	Numbers	Jer	Jeremiah
Deut	Deuteronomy	Lam	Lamentations
Josh	Joshua	Ezek	Ezekiel
Judg	Judges	Dan	Daniel
Ruth	Ruth	Hos	Hosea
1-2 Sam	1-2 Samuel	Joel	Joel
1-2 Kgs	1-2 Kings	Amos	Amos
1-2 Chr	1-2 Chronicles	Obad	Obadiah
Ezra	Ezra	Jonah	Jonah
Neh	Nehemiah	Mic	Micah
Esth	Esther	Nah	Nahum
Job	Job	Hab	Habakkuk
Ps/Pss	Psalms	Zeph	Zephaniah
Prov	Proverbs	Hag	Haggai
Eccl	Ecclesiastes	Zech	Zechariah
(or Qoh)	(or Qoheleth)	Mal	Malachi

[1]This material comes from P. H. Alexander, et al., *The SBL Handbook of Style* (Peabody, MA: Hendrickson, 1999) 71–4. I have reformatted and edited the text slightly.

Books of the Apocrypha

Bar	Baruch	Jdt	Judith
Add Dan	Additions to Daniel	1-2 Macc	1-2 Maccabees
Pr Azar	Prayer of Azariah	3-4 Macc	3-4 Maccabees
Bel	Bel and the Dragon	Pr Man	Prayer of Manasseh
Sg Three	Song of the Three Young Men	Ps 151	Psalm 151
Sus	Susanna	Sir	Sirach/Ecclesiasticus
1-2 Esd	1-2 Esdras	Tob	Tobit
Add Esth	Additions to Esther	Wis	Wisdom of Solomon
Ep Jer	Epistle of Jeremiah		

Books of the New Testament

Matt	Matthew	1-2 Thess	1-2 Thessalonians
Mark	Mark	1-2 Tim	1-2 Timothy
Luke	Luke	Titus	Titus
John	John	Phlm	Philemon
Acts	Acts	Heb	Hebrews
Rom	Romans	Jas	James
1-2 Cor	1-2 Corinthians	1-2 Pet	1-2 Peter
Gal	Galatians	1-2-3 John	1-2-3 John
Eph	Ephesians	Jude	Jude
Phil	Philippians	Rev	Revelation
Col	Colossians		

C. What were God's weapons?

D. What sort of God is described here? Which of the Mesopotamian deities does this description of God most resemble?

Psalm 74:12–17

A. Who was God's opponent?

B. What did God do with his opponent after defeating it?

Psalm 89:5–13

A. What was God's position in the cosmos?

B. Who was God's opponent?

C. What did God do with his opponent after defeating it?

Psalm 104:1–13, 24–26

A. What was God's mode of transport?

B. What did God do after defeating the foe?

C. How is God described here?

Analysis

A. List at least three similarities between the Eneuma Elis and the Biblical material.

B. List at least three differences between the Eneuma Elis and the Biblical material.

*C. How would you explain the fact that there are both so many similarities and so many differences? (Note: Be *creative,* brainstorm, and let your thoughts roam freely. Your explanation needs to account for all the data, but there are different possible explanations.)

*D. How do the answers your friend or roommate provided compare to the descriptions found in Habbakuk or Psalms?

IMPLICATIONS

There are two important implications from this material. First, the Hebrew Bible shares the cosmology or world-view of other Ancient Near Eastern civilizations. This suggests that studying other ancient texts may help clarify the Bible.

Second, and more important, our cosmology is *not* that of the Ancient Near East or the Bible. We live in a post-Enlightenment, scientific world. For most people, the scientific world-view explains planetary motion, how people get sick and can be healed, why rain, earthquakes, and other natural phenomena occur, and many other facets of their lives. The ancients had very different explanations for all of these, as we will see as we read through the Hebrew Bible and New Testament.

Hence, when we read the Bible, we read a text that (for some of us) is very familiar but at the same time is very alien since we all live in a post-Enlightenment world. This is one of the reasons the Bible is difficult to read: we have to struggle to understand what it is saying, since it uses a different language to describe the cosmos, a language of mythic truth, rather than scientific truth.

By "mythic," religious scholars do not mean "false." Rather, myths allow humans to describe the indescribable. We are burdened by human language, designed to explain the human world. Religious visionaries have always had difficulty articulating their experiences of the divine because human language is not suited to describe the divine realm (see, for example, how Ezekiel struggles to describe God's throne chariot in Ezekiel 1 or how Arjuna tries to describe Krishna in the eleventh teaching of the Bhagavad-Gita).

Religious teachers have always known that myths are simultaneously true and false. They are *historically* false (or at least unverifiable), but *mythically* true. Jesus (as we will see) taught in parables. Jesus and his audiences knew the parables were historically false but they revealed more important mythic truths about God, God's compassion for humanity, or the coming Kingdom of God.

The differences between the ancient and modern world view is humorously illustrated in Monty Python's *Life of Brian* when Brian tries to teach a crowd using parables.[1]

BRIAN: Ohh. Look. There was this man, and he had two servants.
ARTHUR: What were they called?
BRIAN: What?
ARTHUR: What were their names?
BRIAN: I don't know. And he gave them some talents.
EDDIE: You don't know?!
BRIAN: Well, it doesn't matter!
ARTHUR: He doesn't know what they were called!
BRIAN: Oh, they were called "Simon" and "Adrian." Now—
ARTHUR: Oh! You said you didn't know!
BRIAN: It really doesn't matter. The point is there were these two servants—
ARTHUR: He's making it up as he goes along.

The humor of the scene comes from the fact that the audience is asking *modern* questions—"What were the names of the servants?"—rather than listening like an ancient audience, which would have recognized the parable form and known that the point was *mythic truth* rather than literal or historic truth.

Unfortunately, most modern readers are like Brian's audience: we are so stuck in modernity and post-Enlightenment definitions of truth that we do not recognize the truth of myth. To appreciate the Bible, however, we must struggle against the idea that "true" is only "historically verifiable." Truth is a large and complex category in religious studies.

---

[1]Text taken from Adam R. Jones' transcription from the film, available at http://www.mwscomp.com/movies/brian/brian.htm.

FOR FURTHER READING

John Day, "Dragon and Sea, God's Conflict with," *Anchor Bible Dictionary (ABD)* 2: 228–31.

W. G. Lambert, "Enuma Elish," *ABD* 2: 526–28.

Lowell K. Handy, "Marduk," *ABD* 4: 522–523.

CHAPTER 3

The Genesis Creation and Flood Narrative(s)

Read Gen 1:1–2:25, 6:1–8:22.

In this chapter we will:

- Be introduced to the methodology of *Source Criticism*
- Read the more familiar versions of creation found in the Bible
- Think about how these descriptions of creation are related to the ones we looked at in the previous chapter

SOURCE CRITICISM

The basic assumption of source criticism is that the Bible was not written by a single author at a single time. At times, biblical authors make this clear. Many times in 1 and 2 Kings, after describing the reign of a particular king, the author says:

> Now the rest of the deeds of King So-and-so, are they not written in the Book of the Chronicles of the Kings of Israel? (1 Kg 14:19, 14:29, 15:7, 15:23, 15:31, etc.)

In addition to these explicit notices of a biblical author using older sources, there are reasons to believe that other sections of the Bible also derive from multiple sources. This idea is contentious, especially with the five books traditionally attributed to Moses, called Torah or Pentateuch.

But source critics suggest that there are reasons to doubt that one author wrote the Torah. Many times the same story is told twice (*doublets*), in other places the style and/or vocabulary shifts markedly, and yet other passages seem to reflect later events (*anachronisms*).

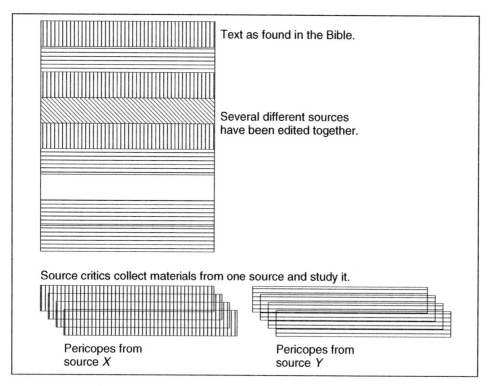

Figure 3–1. Source criticism takes pericopes or sections of text, writes them down on index cards, sorts the cards into stacks with similar characteristics, and then studies each stack to discern who might have written it and why. What are the source's goals, bias, or theology?

Source criticism attempts to sort out these puzzles by

1. Isolating sections of text (called *pericopes*)
2. Sorting the *pericopes* into groups that have the same characteristics (such as ways of describing God, particular interests, or theology)
3. Attempting to figure out which group (or *source*) was written first, which second, and so forth.

Source criticism is a very powerful technique for historians. For example, if a historian wanted to try to trace the history of Israelite worship and theology, she could examine all the sources she thought were early and compare them to later sources.

Many scholars think the stories about creation and the flood found in Genesis may be fruitfully examined with source criticism.

The Creation Narrative(s)

Read Gen 1:1–2:4a (the first half of verse 4 of chapter 2) and fill in your answers in column two. Then read Gen 2:4b–2:25 and fill in the third column.

TABLE 3–1

	Creation Story A: Genesis 1:1-2:4a	Creation Story B: Genesis 2:4b-25
1. What is the name of the Creator in this account?		
2. How long did it take for the Creator to complete the task of creation (in days)?	See 2:2.	See 2:4b.
3. From what original "stuff" did the Creator make the world?	See 1:2.	See 2:5, 2:7.
4. In what order or sequence did creation take place? Number and list the order.		
5. How is the creation of the humans described?	See 1:27.	See 2:7, 2:21-22.
6. What is the task of the human creatures?	See 1:26, 28-30.	See 2:15-17, 19-20.
7. The Hebrew word *ruah* means "breath," "wind," or "spirit."	How is *ruah* used in 1:2?	How is *ruah* used in 2:7?
8. The Hebrew world *'adam* means "mankind," or "humanity."	How is *'adam* used in 1:27?	How is *'adam* used in 2:7-8?
9. By what means does the Creator cause things to come into being?		

Chart based on C.B. Marshall, *A Guide Through the Old Testament* (Louisville: Westminster/John Knox Press, 1989), p. 23.

The Divine Name

In row 1 of Table 3–1, you noticed that the creator deity of the Bible is referred to in two different ways. It appears in Genesis 1 as God and in Genesis 2 as LORD. What is the difference?

In Hebrew, there are several different words used to refer to deity/deities. The generic word for a deity is *el;* for deities (plural) it is *elohim.* The biblical authors used both the singular and plural forms to refer to their deity and used the same terms to refer to the deities of their neighbors. English translators translate both singular and plural forms as *God* if they think it refers to Israel's deity; they translate it as *god* or *gods* if they think it refers to a non-Israelite deity.

In addition to the generic term for deity, the Israelites' deity also had a proper name (like Zeus or Thor). Scholars believe it was probably pronounced *Yahweh.* In English translations the divine name is rendered as LORD.

So the two different terms for the creator deity found in English translations reflect differences in the underlying Hebrew.

---

*A. Why might scholars think there are two different accounts of how God created the world in Gen 1 and 2? Do you think they are correct? Why or why not?

*B. If you wanted to describe God (i.e., what does God look like? what are God's abilities or attributes?) what would you say, based on Genesis 2?

*C. What would you say, based on Genesis 1?

Figure 3–2. The creation of humanity is depicted on the central arch above the western doors of the National Cathedral in Washington, DC. Entitled *Ex Nihilio,* it depicts eight figures emerging from a swirling cloud. Is this how humans are created in Genesis?

The Flood Narrative(s)

Carefully read Genesis 6:1–8:22 to fill out the second and third columns of Table 3–2. Note that this is more difficult than the creation worksheet, because the two flood accounts are spliced together and it can be hard to differentiate between them. To help you, I have included biblical citations for each box.

TABLE 3–2

	Flood Story A	Flood Story B
1. What prompts God to destroy life on earth?	Gen 6:11	Gen 6:5
2. How many animals go onto the ark?	6:19, 7:9	7:2
3. When did the flood begin?	7:6, 11	
4. How long did the flood continue?	7:24	7:12,17, 8:6
5. When did the flood end?	8:13–14	
6. Where did the Ark come to rest?	8:4	
7. How did the man know when to open the Ark?	8:7	8:8
8. What did the man do after the flood?		8:20–22
9. What is the name of the deity in these verses?		

*A. Why might some scholars think there two different flood stories were combined by a later redactor? Do you think this idea is correct? Why or why not?

Analysis

Most scholars think Creation Story A and Flood Story A (CSA, FSA) derive from the same source. Creation Story B and Flood Story B (CSB, FSB) derive from a different source.

*A. If you look at Tables 3–1 and 3–2, what similarities can you discern between CSA and FSA?

SPOTLIGHT ON SCHOLARSHIP: Sources of the Pentateuch

Richard Elliot Friedman has written an accessible description of the results of source criticism [Richard Elliot Friedman, *Who Wrote the Bible?* (San Francisco: HarperSanFrancisco, 1997)]. In it, he presents his arguments about the different sources or strands that comprise the Pentateuch.

Friedman argues that there are four main sources of the Pentateuch: J, E, D, and P.

The two oldest strands are J and E. J is called "J" because it refers to God as Yahweh (or "Jahweh" in German, where source criticism was developed). J describes God anthropomorphically (as in the Eden story) and provides a universal history, starting with creation, which focuses on Israel's origins and divine election. J is especially interested in stories that take place in the southern kingdom, Judah. For this reason, Friedman argues it was composed in Judah.

E is called "E" because it refers to God using the generic term "Elohim" (see "Divine Name" on page 16). E describes God as more remote, communicating with people via dreams or angelic messengers. E is interested in stories that take place in the northern kingdom, Israel, and thus, was probably composed there. Friedman argues that E was critical of the religious practices of both Israel and Judah, suggesting that the author was not a priest.

Dating J and E is difficult. Other scholars date J to the United Monarchy (around 950 BCE) and E a century later. Friedman is more vague, presenting a range of dates for each source: J, between 840 and 722 BCE, and E, between 922 and 722 BCE.

At some point the two oldest sources were combined into JE, which some scholars call the *epic* (or *old epic*) text. Since the J strand is better preserved than E, it is likely that it was combined by Judahite editors, who favored their local stories over the northern stories. These were probably brought south by refugees from Israel, fleeing the destruction of their kingdom in 722 BCE.

The third strand is called D, which stands for Deuteronomy. D was not combined with any other source and stands on its own as the book of Deuteronomy. The date of its composition is unclear, but predates the reforms of Josiah (ca. 630 BCE), since finding the Book of the Law (which most scholars believe is Deuteronomy) was the catalyst for Josiah's reformation.

The last strand of the Pentateuch is the Priestly source. Friedman argues that P was written before 609 BCE as an alternative to JE. The P source emphasizes topics important to priests, such as cultic practices, Law, Aaron (the founder of the priesthood), and genealogies. It portrays God without the anthropomorphisms of J or the dreams and dialogues of E. P's God is a distant, disembodied force (as in Gen 1).

Sometime after the exile (which ended in 538 BCE), someone skillfully stitched JE and P together. This is ironic, Friedman argues, because P is a polemic *against* JE and the two traditions disagree in many places. To this was added D (Deuteronomy) to produce the Pentateuch as we know it.

Some of Friedman's suggestions—such as his desire to provide authors for D and the final redactor—have not met universal acceptance. As noted above, other scholars date J and E differently. Still others place P in the exilic or post-exilic periods. But Friedman's basic arguments are close to the scholarly consensus regarding multiple sources in the Pentateuch.

*B. How about for CSB and FSB?

*C. Which one do you think is older? Why?

FOR FURTHER READING

John Barton, "Source Criticism: Old Testament," *Anchor Bible Dictionary* (*ABD*) 6:162–65.
Robert A. Oden, Jr, "Cosmogony, Cosmology," *ABD* 1:1162–71.

CHAPTER 4

Primordial History (Gen 1–11)

Read Gen 1–11 (you may want to skim or even skip the genealogies, such as Gen 4:7–26, 5, 10, and 11:10–32).

In this chapter, we will:

- Learn about literary criticism
- Look for formal structures in these texts
- Introduce some recurring themes found in the Bible

We have used source criticism to examine Genesis 1–2 and 6–8 in the previous two worksheets. This chapter will examine two other narratives in this portion of the biblical text using literary methodology.

LITERARY CRITICISM

Literary methods tend to ignore questions of sources to focus closely on the received text. Literary approaches do not (usually) deny multiple authors for various biblical texts, but choose to examine the literary artistry exhibited by the text in its present form. This sort of biblical study resembles the study of other literature, ancient or modern. Scholars may study:

- How specific words (*Leitwört*) are used, often repetitively, with specific characters
- How certain ideas or images recurr to create a **motif**
- How certain motifs or words appear repeatedly forming a **theme**
- How some themes ocurr so often that they can be identified as **type-scenes**—scenes that we expect to have certain features or actions

We will examine each of these different ideas as we go through the Bible.

Biblical literary scholars are also often interested in formal structures embedded in the biblical texts. These structures are sequences of ideas that provide an overarching shape to the stories. Two patterns frequently employed by biblical authors are *chiasmus* and *parallelism*.

A *chiasmus* (plural: *chiasmi*, adj: *chiastic*) exhibits symmetry around a point in the narrative, but the second part is reversed. This is typically diagrammed in the following manner:

A: Abel was a keeper of sheep.
   B: And Cain a tiller of the ground.
   B′: Cain brought to the Lord an offering. . .
A′: And Abel brought of the firstlings of his flock. . . (Gen 4:2b–4a)

In this simple *chiasmus*, A and A′ (read "A-prime") are connected by a common subject (Abel), and B and B′ are connected by a different common subject (Cain). We will see more complex *chiasmi* when we study Jacob and Joshua.

A *parallelism* (or *parallel* form) has a sequence of events (A, B, C) that are repeated (A′, B′, C′) in parallel. An example:

A: God speaks to Jonah (Jonah 1:1)   A′: God speaks to Jonah again (3:1)
B: Jonah runs from Nineveh (1:3)   B′: Jonah travels to Nineveh (3:3)
C: Jonah speaks to gentiles (1:9)   C′: Jonah speaks to gentiles (3:4)
D: Gentiles worship God/Yahweh   D′: Gentiles repent & seek forgiveness
(1:14–16)   (3:6–9)
E: God uses nature to help Jonah (1:17)   E′: God uses nature to help Jonah (4:6)
F: Jonah prays to God (2:1–9)   F′: Jonah prays to God (4:2–3, 8b)

As in the chiastic structure, the different elements (A, A′; B, B′; etc.) are connected by common subjects, themes, or actions.

The Tower of Babel (11:1–9)

A. This story has a strongly parallel structure. Write down what happens in each of these verses:

   1:                          6:

   3:                          7:

   4:                          8:

B. What is the *etiological*[1] function of this story?

---

[1]An *etiology* provides an explanation for why things are the way they are.

THEMES

It is easy to focus on the minutiae of the Bible and not notice overarching ideas. We "can't see the forest because of the trees." To address this problem, we will be considering several *themes* or *motifs* that recur in the Bible, but that may be scattered in different places. These themes will include National Origins, Covenants, and The Promised Land.

Societies have often relied on the Bible to explain or justify various societal relationships. Hence, we will also consider several themes of contemporary interest, including Gender Roles, and Slavery and the Poor.

It will be important to focus on what the biblical text says, rather than what we *think* or even "know" it says. Many of these themes are deceptively familiar. As we have seen, everyone knows God is merciful and abounding in steadfast love, but fewer are aware that the Bible also describes God using language of a warrior deity, driving a storm-chariot, and battling sea monsters.

Theme: Gender Roles

People (usually men) sometimes justify ideas of female inferiority by referring to the Bible, since "the woman was created second and she is the one who disobeys God."

A. What was the sequence in which humans were created in Genesis 1?

B. How about in Genesis 2?

C. When were animals created in each story?

D. Does the Bible support the idea that the creation sequence suggests superiority?

E. Where was the man when the woman is talking to the snake and eating the fruit of the tree of knowledge?

F. Who told the truth about the effects of eating of the tree of knowledge, Yahweh or the snake?

G. In what way did the Serpent "trick" the women (Gen 3:13)?

H. Sometimes we hear of a young child who finds a gun in the home and accidentally shoots a sibling or friend. When this happens, who is responsible?

I. Can we draw a parallel with the Garden of Eden? If so, who is responsible for the humans' eating from the tree of knowledge?

Theme: Slavery

In 1856, Thomas Stringfellow penned the following:

> The first recorded language which was ever uttered in relation to slavery, is the inspired language of Noah. In God's stead he says, "Cursed be Canaan;" "a servant of servants shall he be to his brethren." "Blessed be the Lord God of Shem; and Canaan shall be his servant." "God shall enlarge Japheth, and he shall dwell in the tents of Shem; and Canaan shall be his servant." Gen. ix: 25, 26, 27. Here, language is used, showing the favor which God would exercise to the posterity of Shem and Japheth, while they were holding the posterity of Ham in a state of abject bondage. May it not be said in truth, that God decreed this institution before it existed; and has he not connected its existence with prophetic tokens of special favor, to those who should be slave owners or masters? He is the same God now, that he was when he gave these views of his moral character to the world; and unless the posterity of Shem and Japheth, from whom have sprung the Jews, and all the nations of Europe and America . . . God decreed slavery—and shows in that decree, tokens of good-will to the master.[1]

A. Read Gen 9:18-28. Who did Noah curse?

Read Gen 10:6. Some of Ham's offspring populated Africa: Cush (Nubia or Ethiopia), Egypt, and Put (Libya or N. Africa).

B. Does Noah's curse legitimate enslavement of Africans, or is Stringfellow misreading the Bible?

[1]Thornton Stringfellow, *Scriptural and Statistical Views in Favor of Slavery* (Richmond, VA: J. W. Randolph, 1856). Document available from http://docsouth.unc.edu/church/string/menu.html.

FOR FURTHER READING

Edward L. Greenstein, "Wordplay, Hebrew," *Anchor Bible Dictionary* 6: 968–971.
Muhammad A. Dandamayev, "Slavery: Old Testament," *ABD* 6: 62–65.
Frank Anthony Spina, "Babel (Place)," *ABD* 1:561–63.

CHAPTER 5

Patriarchs and Matriarchs Family Tree

Many students find keeping track of the different members of Abraham's family confusing. Filling out the following family tree will clarify their relationships.

On this chart, an equal sign (=) indicates marriage. An equal sign with a "c" above it indicates marriage (or at least intercourse) with a maidservant or concubine. Numbers indicate birth sequence, which is important, since older sons were supposed to inherit more than their brothers.

Abraham's Family

Read the following passage and complete the chart below.

Gen 11:27–30, 16:15–16, 24:62–67, 25:19–27

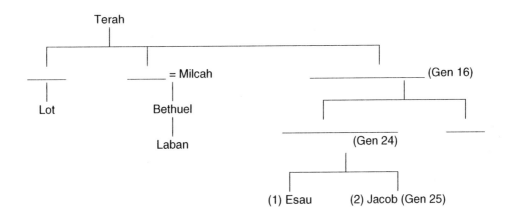

Jacob's Family

The sequence in which Jacob's children is born is significant. I have provided numbers—fill in the names.

Gen 29:31–30:25; 35:16–18

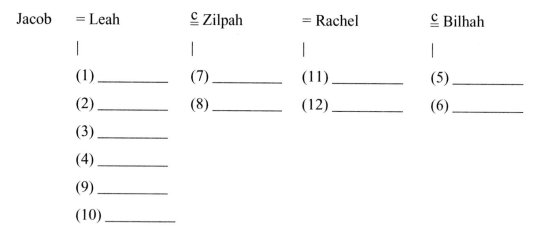

Jacob = Leah $\underline{c}$ Zilpah = Rachel $\underline{c}$ Bilhah

        | | | |

(1) _____   (7) _____   (11) _____   (5) _____

(2) _____   (8) _____   (12) _____   (6) _____

(3) _____

(4) _____

(9) _____

(10) _____

Map 5–1.

Now look at Map 5–1 on p. 26, which shows the location of the various tribes. Note: Joseph isn't on the map—his place is taken by his sons, Manasseh and Ephraim (see Gen 48:1–7).

*A. What correlation can you find between the sequence in which Jacob's descendants are born and their locations on the map? How about correlations between who the mother is and the tribe's location on the map?

*B. What might this suggest about *when* Jacob's family tree was developed?

CHAPTER 6

Abraham

Read Gen 12-23; selection from Homer's *Odyssey,* book 19 (appendix, page 000).

In this chapter, we will:

- Study the Abraham cycle using narrative analysis
- Think about Hebrew literary style
- Explore several important *themes*

Narrative Tension

In the Abraham cycle, tension is created when God makes promises to Abraham. The question for the reader is "when will these promises be fulfilled?" (or perhaps even, "will these promises be fulfilled?") Abraham seems to have struggled with these questions as well and these struggles propel his story—a continual effort to see the promises fulfilled.

A. God promises two things in his covenants with Abraham (Gen 15:1–21, 17:1–14). What are they?

1.

2.

B. Which one does Abraham seem more concerned about?

C. How do Abraham and Sarah initially try to deal with the tension (see Chapter 16)?
   Do they successfully resolve the tension? Why or why not?

D. Does the birth of Isaac resolve the tension? Why or why not?

E. What finally *does* resolve the tension?

Theme: National Origins

We discussed above the curse of Canaan. Noah cursed his grandson Canaan because Ham, Canaan's father, "saw the nakedness of his father" (Noah) (Gen 9:22). Some scholars have speculated that this denotes some sexual act. The idea that biblical authors described their neighbors as descending from people involved in illicit sexual activities can be seen in three stories in the Abraham cycle. Consider the following examples:

Moab (Gen 19:30–38):

Ammon (Gen 19:30–38):

Ishmael (Gen 21:9—the word translated as "playing" here is translated as "fondling" in Gen 26:8, which might explain Sarah's strongly negative reaction to Ishmael):

As we will see, Israel had many conflicts with these peoples, so it is not surprising that they had hostile attitudes towards them. It is a safe bet that each of these peoples had different stories to explain their national origins!

Hebrew Literary Style

The binding of Isaac is perhaps the most important event in Abraham's life for later Jews: it was frequently depicted in ancient synagogue art. Because of its importance, we will look at it closely and also use it as a case-study to compare Greek and Hebrew epic literature.

Read the selection from Homer's *Odyssey* (appendix, pp. 296–297).

A. Highlight or underline the portions of the selection that are dialogue or speech.
   How large a portion of the selection have you highlighted?

B. How did Ulysses get his name?

C. How did Autolycus' sons prepare the feast for Ulysses?

D. How did neither the dogs nor the men notice the boar?

E. What happened when Euryclea saw Ulysses' scar?

F. How did Ulysses prevent Euryclea from alerting Penelope?

Figure 6–1. This panel of mosaic floor greeted worshippers as they entered the sixth century CE synagogue at Beit Alpha in Galilee. On the left are Abraham's servants with the donkey. On the right is the altar, with Isaac to its upper left. Abraham holds the knife, prepared to slaughter Isaac. God's intervention is symbolized by the hand sticking out of a cloud. In the center of the panel is the ram, tangled in the thicket, who is sacrificed in Isaac's place. The panel's prominent location in the synagogue indicates the importance of the story for ancient Jews.

Read Gen 22:1–19, the binding of Isaac.

A. What does Abraham think about God's request? What does he think about while ascending Mt. Moriah? How about Isaac?

B. Why did God decide to test Abraham in this manner?

C. Highlight or underline sections of dialogue or speech. Approximately how much of the selection have you underlined?

*List at least two differences between Greek and Hebrew epic literature.

Without using lush narrative description, biblical authors are able to convey important information very concisely, although not always unambiguously. Consider the following:

A. How is Abraham's love of Isaac indicated in this narrative? Does God acknowledge this love?

B. Repeated elements and changes to repeated elements can often provide important clues to understand characters better.

   1. What does the author emphasize about their relationship as they approach the mountain?

   2. God called to Abraham in verses 1 and 11 and he responds each time. How are these calls and responses different? What is the biblical author stressing by making them different?

C. How has Abraham's character changed from earlier (Gen 16) to later (Gen 22)?

D. The Bible's terse narrative style is frequently ambiguous, encouraging readers to "fill in the blanks." This can be seen here, where God's words (vss. 12b and 16b) are unclear enough that some medieval rabbis thought that Abraham killed Isaac, but that God subsequently resurrected him. Why might they think this? (Hint: see also vss. 13 and 19)

Erich Auerbach argued in the first chapter of _Mimesis_ (Princeton: Princeton University Press, 1953) that the differences between Homeric epic and Hebrew epic related to their goals and world view. Auerbach argued that Homer was primarily for entertainment: it is intellectually satisfying, carefully describing characters, their thoughts and motives, their clothing and surroundings, and their activities. It uses grammatically complex syntax and rich vocabulary. All the characters are either deities or elite humans. It is legend and fantasy. And Homer and his audience knew it.

Biblical authors thought they were writing history. Some legendary material appears at times (for example, miraculous stories, like David's defeat of Goliath), but much more appears to be history. In the stories about David (in 2 Samuel), God appears infrequently while human actors (David, Saul, Absalom, and others), with their conflicting motivations, come to the fore. The authors of the Bible believed they were writing Truth, using simple language. But their lack of description, which obscures of motivation for both humans and God, forces readers to struggle to interpret it. Auerbach argues that one cannot just sit back and passively enjoy the Bible, as you can with Homer.

One of the consequences of these different goals is that Homer's characters are static, both in personality and in age. Their situations change little—Odysseus wanders for years, but neither ages nor changes. Auerbach argues that, because the Biblical authors had a sense of history, their characters change over time. Abraham, Jacob, and others are different at the end of the story than they are at the beginning.

You can think about this for yourself. Do you think Abraham changes and develops over time? You may want to think about this when reading about Jacob, Joseph, Moses, David, and other Biblical heroes.

Theme: Promised Land

God's covenant with Abraham included offspring and land. But which land? What are its boundaries? In some places, it is not clearly described. Read Gen 13:14–15, 17 and Gen 17:8.

A. What are the boundaries of the Promised Land?

In other places, a clearer description is offered. Read Gen 15:18–21.

B. What are the boundaries of the Promised Land?

C. What nations are living there and will be displaced?

FOR FURTHER READING

A. R. Miller, "Abraham (Person)," _Anchor Bible Dictionary_ 1: 35–41.

CHAPTER 7

Jacob

Read Gen 24–35, 38.

In this chapter we will:

- Examine a "type scene"
- Study how the Biblical author develops characters

TYPE-SCENES

Source critics argue that duplicate stories or doublets are evidence of multiple sources. For example, Abraham twice tells local leaders that Sarah is his sister. She marries the king, but before they have intercourse, the truth is revealed and Abraham is rewarded for his duplicity (Gen 12:10–20, 20:1–18). Isaac does the same thing with Rebekah (Gen 26:1–11).

Alternately, doublets could reflect a type-scene. We expect certain formula in all forms of literature. In buddy-films (such as *Butch Cassidy and the Sundance Kid, Thelma and Louise, Easy Rider*), we expect a pair of same-sex characters to travel, philosophize, and eventually die violently. In westerns (even revisionary westerns, such as *Unforgiven*), we expect a climatic shoot-out. Similarly, in ancient literature, some scenes are highly formulaic.

Robert Alter argued that betrothal scenes are a good example of type-scenes. He identified several elements common to betrothals: (1) bridegroom (or surrogate) travels to distant land, (2) he meets a girl or girls at a well, (3) water is drawn from the well, (4) the girl/girls run home to announce the stranger, (5) betrothal announced, often with a meal.[1]

---

[1] R. Alter, *The Art of Biblical Narrative* (New York: Basic Books, 1981), 52.

Biblical authors modified these conventions selectively as a way of providing insight into their characters. We will see this by comparing the betrothal scenes of Jacob and Isaac (Gen 24:10–61 and 29:1–20).

TABLE 7–1

	Gen 24:10–61	Gen 29:1–20
1. Who travels?		
2. Where is the well?		
3. Who draws the water?		
4. What is notable about the drawing of water?	See Gen 24:18, 20.	See Gen 29:10.
5. Why are the stories so different in length?		

A. When you compare lines 1 and 3 in Table 7–1, what is notable about the following characters?

1. Isaac

2. Jacob

3. Rebekah

B. What does the style of story (reflected in line 5) suggest about Jacob's character as opposed to Isaac's or perhaps his grandfather, Abraham's?

Characterization

We saw in Chapter 6 that one major stylistic difference between Hebrew and Greek epics was the preference for dialogue found in Hebrew literature. Because of this, we should pay special attention to a person's first words, since they often provide insight into their character.

Jacob and Esau are conceived and born in Genesis 25:19–28. Their first words are found in verses 29–34.

A. How would you describe Esau's words in verses 30 and 32?

B. How would you describe Jacob's words in verses 31 and 33?

C. What might the biblical author be suggesting about them by presenting them in this manner?

Isaac's Blessing

Read Genesis 27. The story of how Isaac blessed Jacob again shows the biblical author's preference for dialogue over narrative.

A. Rebekah overhears Isaac's request of Esau and repeats it to Jacob. How is her repetition different from the original? Are the differences significant? Why?

B. Who is responsible for deceiving Isaac? Is this consistent with the character's other activities?

C. Is Isaac suspicious? How is he fooled?

D. How are the characterizations of Rebekah and Isaac consistent with the story of their betrothal?

Formal Narrative Structure

The Bible was composed in a multi-step process. Source criticism has established that different parts of the Bible come from different times, places, and authors. These disparate sources have been skillfully assembled into the present form of the biblical text by a skilled editor. The subtlety and skill of the later editor can be seen by noticing the overarching formal structure constructed for the stories of the patriarchs and matriarchs.

The Jacob cycle exhibits a chiastic pattern, centered on the birth of his children (29:31–30:24). I found several similar elements; see if you can identify more. *Hint*: Start at the center (E) and work outwards; what event(s) before and after (E) parallel one another? Be sure to include biblical citations to facilitate discussion.

A.
  B.
    C.
     D.
       E. Birth of Jacob's children (29:31–30:24)
     D'.
    C'.
  B'.
A'.

Theme: Gender Roles and Deception

Some people cite the Bible to support the idea that women are tricky and deceptive, as with Rebekah. But if we read more widely, a different pattern emerges.

A. What impressed Laben about Abraham's messenger in Chapter 24? What echoes do we have of this aspect of Laben's character in his dealings with Jacob?

B. How did Laben trick Jacob? (Notice the parallel to Jacob's deception of Isaac) (See Chapter 29)

C. How did Jacob later trick Laben? (See Chapter 30)

D. How did Rachel deceive Laben? (See Chapter 31)

E. How did Jacob react to his sons tricking Shechem and Hamor? (See Chapter 34)

F. Why did Jacob respond so differently to this trick than to the previous ones?

G. How did Tamar trick Judah? (See Chapter 38)

H. Why did Tamar trick Judah?

*I. When do characters in the Bible resort to trickery? What prompts them to attempt to deceive one another?

....

FOR FURTHER READING

Stanley D. Walters, "Jacob Narrative," *Anchor Bible Dictionary (ABD)* 3: 599–608.
Robert Martin-Achard, "Isaac (Person)," *ABD* 3: 462–70.

CHAPTER 8

Joseph

Read Gen 37, 39–47.

In this chapter we will:

- Think about how the biblical author used symbols to enhance the main narrative line
- Study one of the longest narrative sequences in Genesis, using literary techniques

The last 13 chapters of Genesis are sometimes called the Joseph *novella*. It is a *novella* (short novel) because its narrative line is continuous and lengthy. It is apparent that the J and E strands have been combined to produce the received text. There are many incongruities that derive from older versions of the story:

- Who was responsible for saving Joseph from his brothers? Reuben (37:21) or Judah (37:26)?
- What was the nationality of the caravan that took Joseph to Egypt—Ishmaelites (37:25) or Midianites (37:28)?

But rather than look at the book from a source critical perspective, we will focus on a literary analysis of the received text. We will see that the story of Joseph forms a unified whole, one that is a masterpiece of Hebrew narrative.

Setting the Stage

Read Chapter 37.

Family Tensions

A. Why did Joseph's brothers resent him?

B. Where have we seen this before? What were the results in previous cases?

C. What do Joseph's brothers do because of their resentment? How does this parallel earlier cases?

Narrative tension—Joseph's two dreams

A. What do Joseph's dreams portend?

B. Who is able to interpret or understand the dream?

C. At the end of the chapter, how likely does it seem that the dreams will become reality?

Clothing as symbol

We noted that the biblical authors avoid descriptive language in their stories. So when we find an object being described, we should take special note of it—the author is signaling something to us. For this reason, as we go through the Joseph story, we will pay special attention to his clothing.

A. What is special about his clothing in the beginning of the chapter?

B. What happens to the clothing at the end of the chapter?

Joseph in Egypt

Read chapters 39–41.

Joseph in Potiphor's house

A. What is Joseph's position in Potiphor's house?

B. How does this fulfill Joe's dream? Does it resolve the narrative tension?

C. Why did Potiphor's wife want to "lie" with Joseph?

Notice the sexual disparity implicit in this pericope. Potiphor, like Abraham, Jacob, or Judah (in Gen 38), could have many wives or concubines and/or visit prostitutes without condemnation, but his wife cannot. Biblical law and custom prohibited women from having sex with men other than their husbands, but no such limit was placed on men.

D. How is Joseph's clothing an important symbol here?

Joseph in jail

A. What is Joseph's position in the jail?

B. How does this fulfill Joseph's dreams? Does it resolve narrative tension?

C. Do the dreams come true?

D. How does this affect the narrative tension?

Joseph in command

A. What is different about Pharaoh's dreams than the four earlier dreams?

B. Do the dreams come true? How does this affect narrative tension?

C. What is the position that Joseph has in the kingdom?

D. How was this foreshadowed?

E. How is Joseph's clothing an important symbol?

Joseph's Brothers

Read chapters 42–44. The fact that no mention is made of Joseph's brothers in chapters 39–41 has led some scholars to suggest that the three chapters circulated independently, perhaps adapted from an Egyptian tale, before being incorporated into their present narrative. But these chapters are utterly necessary to explain the next three chapters, which comprise a counterbalance to the earlier three chapters.

Jacob's character

A. Review the worksheet on Jacob (pp. 35–38). How would you describe his character in Chapters 25–34?

B. Describe his character in Chapter 37.

C. How would you describe his character in Chapters 42–43?

D. Look at the way Jacob blesses Joseph's children in Chapter 48. How is this scene characteristic for Jacob?

Joseph's character

A. How would you describe Joseph's character in Chapter 37?

B. Describe his character in 39–41.

C. Describe his character in 42–44.

D. Do Jacob and Joseph change and develop over time, or are their characters static?

The Finale

Read chapter 45 and 47:13–27. Several scholars have suggested that the Joseph story was composed to serve as a bridge between the older patriarchal narratives, set in Canaan, and the Exodus narrative, set in Egypt. The final chapters set the stage for the Exodus story.

Reconciliation

A. Why are Joseph's brother's "dismayed at his presence" (45:3b)?

B. Joseph, in effect, forgives the brothers for their crime (in ch. 37), with a tripartite statement. Write down each part:

v.5b -

v.7 -

v.8 -

....

FOR FURTHER READING

George W. Coats, "Joseph, Son of Jacob," *Anchor Bible Dictionary* 3:976–81.

CHAPTER 9

Prince of Egypt

Read Exodus 1–15. Watch *Prince of Egypt* (Dreamworks, 1998).

In this chapter we will:

- Consider the origins of our knowledge of biblical materials
- Think about how modern ideas influence the reception of ancient stories

One reason the Bible remains important, thousands of years after its composition is that, as "scripture," it stands in a special category. It has long been used as a source of authority and, even in our secular age, people continue to appeal to it in this manner.

Ironically, for many of us, what we "know" about the Bible does not derive from reading the Bible, but from other sources. We will examine this phenomenon by examining Dreamworks' 1998 animated feature film, *Prince of Egypt*. This movie is easier and perhaps more "fun" than Exodus, but is it a reliable reflection of the Bible?

A. List at least three issues or topics that the Bible leaves unclear, but which are clarified by the movie.

1.

2.

3.

4.

5.

B. List the major characters in:

Exodus   *Prince of Egypt*

C. Which characters are added to (or significantly expanded from) the biblical account by the movie? Why were they added or changed?

D. What Biblical material is omitted from the movie? Why?

*E. What is the pattern of the changes / omissions / additions?

F. Analysis

   1. What is the goal of the movie, *Prince of Egypt?*

   2. What is the goal of the Exodus story?

   3. Are these goals the same?

....

FOR FURTHER READING

Dewey M. Beegle, "Moses (Person)," *Anchor Bible Dictionary (ABD)* 4: 909–18.
James K. Hoffmeier, "Egypt, Plagues in," *ABD* 2: 374–78.

CHAPTER 10

Moses

Read Exodus 1–15.

In this chapter we will:

- Consider the use of keywords (*leitwört*) as a method of characterization
- Revisit the betrothal type-scene
- Think about the theological implications of the plagues

LEITWORT

A *leitwört* (literally a "guiding or leading" word, plural *leitwörter*) is a word that is used repetitively by an author, one that can provide a key to interpreting passages. Hebrew words are formed using a three-letter root, to which other letters could be added to make different words. In English, this would be akin to "run," "ran," "will run," and other verb forms, as well as "runner," "running," "runny," and so forth.

This is often lost when translated into English, which has words from different roots that have grown together. For example, the past tense of "go" is "went," but the present-tense of "went" is "wend," which has fallen out of common usage. A "King" is married to a "Queen" and "rules" his "kingdom." In Hebrew, all these words (not just the first and last) are related.

Additionally, in English, it is often considered bad form to use the same word over and over again. So when Biblical authors do use the same word, frequently it is translated with different terms.

We will consider here how biblical authors used *leitwörten* to provide information about characters.

A. What word do the following passages about Jacob have in common?

    1. Gen 28:11, 18

    2. Gen 29:2b–3, 10

    3. Gen 31:45

    4. Gen 35:14

B. Notice that (2) modifies the "typical" betrothal type-scene. How is this appropriate for Jacob's character?

C. Consider the following passages, all related to Moses. What word do they have in common?

    1. Exod 2:10

    2. Exod 2:19

    3. Exod 15:22–25

D. How is this *Leitwört* appropriate for Moses? (*Hint:* consider Exod 7:14–25 and Exod 14)

Betrothal Type-Scene (Exod 2:15b–21)

Moses' betrothal type-scene is *much* shorter than those of Jacob or Isaac. But it contains all the elements:

A. Where does Moses go?

B. Where does he meet Reuel's daughters?

C. What does Moses do for the daughters that differs from the earlier betrothal scenes? (see Chapter 6, section 1). How is this appropriate for Moses' character?

D. How do we know the daughters *ran* back to Reuel?

E. What happens after Moses helps the daughters?

Theme: Promised Land

Review the Abraham chapter (Chapter 6). Whose land did Yahweh promise to Abraham?

What were its boundaries?

Now read Exod 3:8. How is this description different from those in Genesis?

Read Exod 23:20–33. What are the boundaries here?

How does it say the Israelites will come into the land?

What are they to do with the native inhabitants?

Theological Issues

As you read through Exod 7–12, you will find the famous story of the ten plagues suffered by the Egyptians. Read this section carefully and answer the following questions, jotting down biblical citations to support your answers.

A. Read 4:21–23, 7:2–8, 9:15–16, 10:1–2. Why does God inflict the plagues on the Egyptians?

B. Read Exod 4:2–23 7–10, 14. Why does Pharaoh not allow the Israelites to leave? Pay careful attention to the use of active and passive verbs—who is responsible for Pharoah's recalcitrance?

C. Why might the plagues be theologically troubling? What sort of image do they present for God?

FOR FURTHER READING

Dewey M. Beegle, "Moses (Person)," *Anchor Bible Dictionary (ABD)* 4: 909–18.
Nahum M. Sarna, "Exodus, Book of," *ABD* 2: 689–700.

CHAPTER 11

Legal Materials

Read Exod 19–23; Lev 6:8–7:38, 16, 19, 23, 25.

In this chapter, we will:

- Think about the Ten Commandments and the clarity of biblical law
- Consider the cultic system described in Leviticus

Ten Commandments

What Part of "Thou Shall Not. . ."
Do You Not Understand?
—God

A. You may have seen the above text on a highway billboard. What answer do you think the author of the billboard expected to the query from "God"?

B. Write down the Ten Commandments (Exod 20:2–17)

1.   6.

2.   7.

3.   8.

4.   9.

5.   10.

C. Write down (at least) three questions you have about the Ten Commandments or places where they need clarification. (If you can't think of at least three, you are not trying hard enough.)

1.

2.

3.

D. How are the Ten Commandments different from the laws in chapters 21 and 22?

E. Are the laws in chapters 21 and 22 clearer than the Ten Commandments?

*F. Occasionally, people advocate living life "according to the Bible." Assuming you wanted to do this, do you think it would be easy? What might make it difficult?

Most of Exodus after Chapter 20 and all of Leviticus are concerned with cultic issues. How should the tabernacle be built? How should Israel worship its god? We will briefly examine only two topics in these books: the sacrificial system and the cultic calendar. We will ask source critical questions and think about their historical development.

Sacrifices

Leviticus describes a sacrificial system. There are three main types of sacrifices. Fill out Table 11–1 to compare them.

TABLE 11–1

Cite	Name or Type	What is Sacrificed?	Procedure/Who Gets the Sacrifice?
1. Lev 1:1–10; 6:8–13			
2. 3:1–17; 7:11–18, 28–36			
3. 4:27–35; 6:24–30			

*A. Who does the sacrificial system benefit the most? (*Hint:* it isn't God!)

*B. Review the box on the sources of the Pentateuch (p. 18). To which source would a source critic probably attribute these verses?

Figure 11–1. Archaeologists discovered the remains of an altar at Beer-sheba and reconstructed it. Why the altar has "horns" on its corners is unclear (did it provide a place to bind the sacrificial animal?) but common in this region.

Festival Calendars

Compare the festival calendars of Exodus 23 and Leviticus 23 by completing Table 11–2.

TABLE 11–2

Cite	Feast Name	Date	Length	What Do Worshippers Do?
1. Exod 23:15	Unleavened bread	Abib	7 days	Eat unleavened bread. Don't appear empty-handed.
2. 23:16a				
3. 23:16b				
4. Lev 23:3				
5. 23:5				
6. 23:6–8				
7. 23:9–14				
8. 23:15–21				
9. 23:23–25				
10. 23:26–32				See Lev 16.
11. 23:33–36				
12. 23:39–43				

Indicate where the Levitical calendar's festivals correspond to those from Exodus.

*A. Do you think either of these calendars would have been used by nomadic shepherds? Why or why not?

*B. What would a source critic say about the presence of two calendars?

*C. With two calendars, we have three options:

Case I: Leviticus older than Exodus

Case II: Exodus older than Leviticus

Case III: Calendars of same age

Which option do you think is most likely? Why?

*D. What are some of the similarities between the Levitical calendar (Table 11–2) and the sacrificial system (Table 11–1)?

FOR FURTHER READING

Raymond F. Collins, "Ten Commandments," *Anchor Bible Dictionary (ABD)* 6: 383–87.
Gary A. Anderson, "Sacrifice and Sacrificial Offerings: Old Testament," *ABD* 5: 870–86.
Baruch A. Levine, "Leviticus, Book of," *ABD* 4: 311–320.

CHAPTER 12

Numbers

Read Num 3, 11, 13, 18, 21–23, 25, 31.

In this chapter, we will:

- Use source analysis to think about how Numbers was written
- Use literary analysis to consider the stories about Balaam

Numbers, like Exodus, contains two different sorts of materials. We will use source criticism to identify them and ask who could have written them. Review the Sources of the Pentateuch (page 18) before working on this chapter.

Sources

The two sources found in Numbers are the *Epic* (JE) and the *Priestly* (P). Read the following passages and write down which source you think they belong to and why you think so:

A. Num 3:1–39:

B. Num 11:

C. Num 18:

D. Num 21:1–9:

*E. What are some common themes for the JE traditions?

*F. What are some common themes for P?

Story Line

Recall that JE and P were spliced together very skillfully. I have arranged the verses from Chapter 13 in Table 12–1. Notice that each story line could stand on its own.

TABLE 12–1

Verses	Story Line (1)	Verses	Story Line (2)
1. 1–16		17–20	
2. 21–22		23–24	
3. 25–26		27–31	
4. 32a		32b–33	

*Which story line, 1 or 2, do you think comes from the P source? Which comes from the JE source? Why?

Balaam and His Talking Ass

Balaam was a famous seer, not only in Israel but in surrounding regions as well. A non-Israelite inscription from Jordan describes Balaam's vision of a tour of heaven. Balaam in some biblical traditions is almost a comic figure, but others view him negatively. We will look at examples from each tradition to see their contrasting presentations.

A number of commentators have noted that Num 22–23 exhibit a parallel structure, with folkloric triads of actions. To see this, fill out Table 12–2 (all verses are from Numbers).

TABLE 12–2

Balaam and his Ass	Balak and Balaam
1. 22:22–23	1. 23:2–12
2. 22:24–25	2. 23:13–26
3. 22:26–27	3. 23:27–24:12
4. 22:28	4. 22:38, 23:5, 12, 16

A. How are lines 1–3 in Table 12–2 parallel?

Notice how the story is rife with irony:

B. How is Balaam described in Num 24:3b?

C. How appropriate is this description in Num 22:22–27?

D. What does Balaam wish for in Num 22:29?

E. How far away is the wished-for object?

F. What is humorous about Num 22:28–30?

Balaam Revisted

Read Num 25:1–5.

A. Who was responsible for "leading" the Israelites astray?

B. What is the response of Moses?

Read Num 25:6–15.

A. What is the issue in these verses?

B. What is the response of Moses?

C. Is this the same issue as in Num 25:1–5?

D. What would this suggest to a source critic?

Read 31:1–24.

A. Who is the target of Israel's attack in this chapter?

B. In addition to the kings of Midian, who else did they slay (rather surprisingly, in light of Num 24:25 and 22:5)?

C. What is Baalam credited with in these verses?

D. Is this mentioned in Num 25?

E. How is this tradition about Balaam different from those in Num 22–24?

....

FOR FURTHER READING

Jacob Milgrom, "Numbers, Book of," *Anchor Bible Dictionary (ABD)* 4: 1146–55.
Jo Ann Hackett, "Balaam (Person)," *ABD* 1: 569–72.

CHAPTER 13

Deuteronomy

Read Deut 1–7, 12, 20, 28, 34.

In this chapter, we will:

- Think about the goals of Deuteronomy
- Consider the historical development of Israelite theology

Goal of Deuteronomy

Deuteronomy was a singularly effective document: it prompted a significant cultic reform by the Judean King Josiah (640–609 BCE; see below, Chapter 23).

Read Deut 4:25–40; 6:10–15; 7:1–6; 12.

A. What does the author of Deuteronomy fear the Israelites will do in the promised land?

B. Read Deut 20. What does God order the Israelites to do to the native inhabitants of the land? Why?

*C. Based on your answers to A, why does God (or the author of Deut) advocate B?

D. Where are the Israelites supposed to worship, according to Deut 12?

Figure 13–1. Moses was not allowed to enter the Promised Land, but he ascended Mount Nebo to see it before he died. This photograph, taken on Mt. Nebo, shows the view to the west, with the Dead Sea on the left and the Jordan valley on the right.

Motivation

Let us consider how the discovery of the book of Deuteronomy could have prompted Josiah to change Judah's worship practices.

A. Read Deut 4 and 6. What words or phrases appear repeatedly? Why would these words have encouraged Josiah to institute his reform? (See especially 4:34, 37, 38, 5:6, 6:12–13, 21–22.)

B. Read Deut 28. What will God do to the Israelites if they obey? If they disobey?

C. Does the author of Deuteronomy think "the carrot" or "the stick" is more persuasive?

Monotheism?

Judaism is the oldest of the three monotheistic faiths (the others are Christianity and Islam). But were the Israelites monotheistic? Were they *supposed* to be monotheistic?

A. Look up *monotheism* in a dictionary and write the definition here:

B. Read or review Exod 32 and Num 25. Were the Israelite masses monotheistic?

C. Read or review Exod 15:11, Deut 3:23–4:40, 6:10–15. Are the biblical authors exhibiting monotheism?

Do the biblical authors have Moses or God *command* monotheism?

D. Read Deut 5:6–21 (or Exod 20:2–17). Do the Ten Commandments command monotheism?

Read Deut 6:4–9. Note that there is a variety of ways to translate verse 4 (I have changed "the LORD" to "Yahweh" because it makes the different meanings more obvious).

Yahweh is our God, Yahweh alone
Yahweh, our God, is one Yahweh
Yahweh is our God, Yahweh is one

*F. Is this a statement of monotheism? How do the different ways to translate this verse affect its "monotheism"?

FOR FURTHER READING

Moshe Weinfeld, "Deuteronomy, Book of," *Anchor Bible Dictionary (ABD)* 2: 168–183.
John J. Scullion, "God: God in the Old Testament," *ABD* 2:1041–48.

PART TWO

Historical Books

Joshua, Judges, Samuel, Kings, Chronicles, Ezra, Nehemiah

CHAPTER 14

Overview

In the Jewish tradition, the second part of the Bible is called *Prophets*. It includes not only Isaiah, Jeremiah, Ezekiel and shorter books of 12 other prophets, but also the books of Joshua, Judges, 1 and 2 Samuel, 1 and 2 Kings, all of which are considered to be in some sense prophetic. Ezra, Nehemiah, and Chronicles are in the third part of the Bible, *Writings*.

The Christian tradition collects all books that are historical together. Joshua, Judges, Ruth, Samuel and Kings recount the conquest and settlement of the Israelites in the Promised Land, the flourishing of the Israelite kingdom(s), and their eventual destruction and exile by Assyria and Babylon. Chronicles offers a second version of this history and Ezra and Nehemiah describe what happened to the Judeans after the Exile.

We will follow the latter arrangement, although we will delay consideration of Ruth until we consider novellas (Ch. 34).

Since much of this material purports to be history, we will frequently use historical methods. But ancient authors did not have the same concepts of historiography as we do today; frequently, for example, they report conversations to which they were not privy or tell us the thoughts of people or even God. Hence, while we can use historical methodologies on these texts, it is also appropriate to analyze them from a literary perspective. We will do both sorts of analysis on these texts.

We have used a variety of literary methodologies in Part One. Although we mentioned some historical applications of source criticism, we did not actually examine historical issues. Before we do historical analysis, a few words about historical methodology are required.

HISTORICAL METHODOLOGIES

Different historians have different goals. Some may be interested in the political history of Israel and Judah. Others may focus on Israelite cultic practices: how did the Israelites worship, and how did this change over time? Yet others may want to study social issues: what was the status of women (or slaves or other social groups) at various points in Israel's history?

Whatever their goals, historians start out with several basic assumptions:

- The Bible is to be treated as any other ancient source. Note that this is not the way it has been treated for much of Western history. Rather, scripture was different than other literature, since it was attributed to God (or authors inspired by God). To ensure historical reconstructions will be accepted by historians of any religious background (including those who do not regard the Bible as scripture), historians studying the Bible cannot "privilege" or place the Bible in a special category.
- Human nature is fairly constant. People today are about the same as those living in antiquity. Modern folks are noble and venal, motivated by altruism and greed, interested in politics and try to present themselves or their heroes in the best way they can. The same is true of antiquity. We will see that authors in the Bible can be surprisingly frank about their subjects' shortcomings, even when they idolize them.
- All writing has a thesis or goal. No one goes to the trouble of writing if they do not have a point to make. Unfortunately, the thesis is often not made explicit. Newspaper writing, for example, often claims to be "objective," although it is not. Authors cannot report *everything* that happens, so they select what information they think is most relevant.

This last point is true of the Bible as well. One major goal for historical-critical analysis is to figure out the writer's thesis. If the thesis can be discerned, the author's bias may be understood and allowed for. For example, we will see that the Biblical author held King David in very high regard. Because of this, we may view some of the author's comments about relations between David and Saul as of dubious historical veracity, since the author's goal (or bias) is to glorify David, not to report his activities dispassionately.

The ultimate goal of the historical-critical method is to fit all the sources at our disposal (Biblical texts, other ancient Near Eastern sources, archaeological evidence) into a narrative that is consistent with its sources and seems reasonable. A reasonable history fits our expectations of how people act, societies function, and governments rule. Ideally, biblical history should fit into what we know of the history of Egypt, Assyria, Persia, and other ancient civilizations.

A large portion of the Bible (Joshua, Judges, 1 and 2 Samuel, 1 and 2 Kings) describes the history of the Israelites from their entrance into the promised land, discusses their experiences in the land, and ends with the exile of Judah in 586 BCE. Scholars call these books the Deuteronomistic (or Deuteronomic) History (abbreviated DH throughout this textbook).

We will examine this material in some detail, for a variety of reasons:

- One goal for this textbook is to introduce students to important names and characters in the Bible; many of the most important figures are found in the DH.
- When we read other Biblical material (such as the various prophets), we will try to fit them into the historical framework we will establish in Part Two.
- We will study the theology of the DH. Understanding the DH's theology is important because it forms the basis for the theology of post-exilic Judaism. We will also compare the theologies of other Biblical material to that of the DH.
- The DH is largely narrative and is easier to understand than poetic materials, which comprise the bulk of prophetic literature.

Applying historical methods to biblical texts may not be familiar and may be challenging. Many of us place biblical characters on pedestals: who could be as good as David? But the DH is remarkably candid about the flaws of the characters in Israel's history and certainly does not elevate them into the realm of superhuman.

Our primary goal for the DH will be to try to figure out the thesis (and/or goal) of the DH and then think about how this thesis affected the DH's analysis and presentation of Israel's history. But this is not the only methodology one can use to interpret historical works.

We will occasionally use other methods, including source criticism (see the chapters on Judges and 1 Samuel) and redaction criticism (see the Judges and Chronicles chapters). But generally these techniques will be used in service to historical methodology.

A NOTE ON HISTORY (ANCIENT AND MODERN)

The further back we go in history, the fewer "facts" we find preserved. History is a narrative; it does not establish "truth," but probability. For much history, we can never know truth, because not enough material (textual or archaeological) exists to allow us to be 100 percent sure of what actually happened. Many times, historians are presented with sets of conflicting evidence and they must try to sort out what they think is the most likely or probable sequence of events. Hence, historians make up stories (or scenarios) that explain the data they are presented with; they do not establish "truth."

Two biblical examples illustrate this.

How Did Saul Die?

According to 1 Sam 31:3–5, Philistine archers badly wounded Saul. He requested that his armor bearer kill him, but his armor bearer refused. Saul then killed himself, by falling on his own sword. His armor bearer also killed himself.

According to 2 Sam 1:6–10, one of Saul's soldiers found Saul grievously injured, leaning on his spear. Saul asked the soldier to kill him and he did so. He then took Saul's crown and brought it to David.

How did Saul die? We might try to harmonize these stories: perhaps "falling on his sword" did not kill Saul immediately and the soldier found him later, propped up with his spear. The problem is that the stories conflict fundamentally: it is hard to see how Saul could have "killed himself" but not actually died. There is no mention of the soldier finishing the job off. And so forth.

Alternately, we might assume one account is true and see if we can think of a scenario that would explain why someone would make up the other account.

Manasseh

Manasseh is important in 2 Kings, as he is blamed for the exile of the Judahites (2 Kg 21:1–18). The biblical historian tells us that he disobeyed God's directions about proper worship to such an extent that God decided to exile the Judahites. What else he did during his 55-year reign (the longest of any Judean king) is not mentioned.

Manasseh is important in 2 Chronicles as well, as he provides a protypical example for the Judahites. He sinned as recorded in 2 Kings but Chronicles reports that God allowed the Assyrians to capture him and take him into exile. In exile, he repented and beseeched God's forgiveness. God heard him and restored him to Jerusalem, where he got rid of the cultic materials that offended God earlier.

So, was Manasseh captured by the Assyrians and exiled? Did he repent and worship "correctly"? We have two different histories and cannot answer the question definitely. The best we can do is to try to identify the bias or thesis or goal of the authors of 2 Kings and 2 Chronicles. If we can identify their bias, we can ask which author would have been more likely to have omitted important facts about Manasseh or to have made up a story about his exile and repentance.

CHAPTER 15

Historical Sketch

The portion of the Bible to be explored in Part Two covers the period from the conquest (usually dated to around 1100 BCE) to the destruction of Jerusalem and beginning of the exile (in 586 BCE). It concludes with the post-exilic rebuilding of the Jerusalem Temple and activities of returning exiles, around 450 BCE. The Bible focuses on the activities of the Israelites, but to understand their history, we need to have a thumbnail sketch of the larger historical setting.

The land of where Israel and Judah were located, also called Canaan or Palestine, has few natural resources. A ridge of rugged mountains divines the coastal plain from the Jordan rift valley. The regions that are suitable for agriculture are limited.

But Israel and Judah occupied a territory of great strategic importance, as it is part of the land-bridge connecting Egypt to Mesopotamia. These two regions are agriculturally rich and have significant natural resources. It was here that civilization first developed in the Ancient Near East. The empires that developed both north and south of Palestine were interested in controlling it, to maintain a buffer against their enemies. It is for this reason that kingdoms in Mesopotamia and Egypt fought to control the land where the Israelites later settled. From around 2000 to 1200, Palestine was under Egyptian control and formed the province of Canaan.

From around 1250 to 1150 BCE, significant migrations of people took place in the eastern part of the Mediterranean region. These migrants, called sea-people by the Egyptians, invaded Asia Minor and Greece, Crete, Cyprus, and settled along the coast of Canaan, where they were called Philistines. Egypt was not overrun, but defending itself against the invaders cost it a great deal and weakened it to such an extent that it never regained its former status.

During this period of turmoil, the Israelites settled in the mountainous regions of Judah and Israel. (We will discuss the origin of the Israelites and how they were organized when we discuss the book of Judges.)

The Philistines, who settled along the coast, tried to exert control over inland regions where the Israelites lived. The need to defend themselves against the Philistine threat may have prompted the Israelites to move toward a monarchy, as we will see when we discuss Samuel and Saul.

David, who ruled from around 1000 to 960 BCE, united the northern and southern Israelite tribes and took advantage of the weakness of the Egyptian and Mesopotamian superpowers to conquer a large swath of land. His kingdom included parts of modern-day Israel, Jordan, and Syria. David's empire did not last long—parts of it rebelled against his son, Solomon. And after Solomon's death, in 922 BCE, the kingdom split into two parts: the northern kingdom of Israel and the southern kingdom of Judah.

After the dissolution of the united kingdom, Palestine had a number of small kingdoms, including Israel, Judah, Ammon, Syria, Moab, and Edom. These fought amongst themselves and attempted to dominate each other. Egypt remained too weak to exert control over the region.

In Mesopotamia, however, Assyria gained more and more power. Beginning in the ninth century, its authority began to be felt in Palestine, prompting (at times) the local dynasties to form alliances to resist it. These ultimately failed. In 722 BCE the Assyrians besieged Samaria, the capital of Israel, and destroyed it. They took some of the Israelites into exile and settled other people in their place. These exiles are the so-called "Ten Lost Tribes of Israel." The Assyrians also besieged Jerusalem for three years, but were unable to capture the capital of Judah.

Assyria's decline was precipitous. Its conquest of Babylon and Egypt (around 650) prompted national revivals in both regions. In 626 Babylon revolted and established itself as independent; in 612, the Babylonians destroyed Nineveh, the capital of Assyria. Upon the ruins of the Assyrian empire, four smaller kingdoms emerged in its territory: the Medes in Iran, the Neo-Babylonians in Mesopotamia, the Egyptians, and the Lydians in Asia Minor. Again, we will see a correlation between weakness of the superpowers and regional dynasts' attempts to expand, as with Josiah.

The Neo-Babylonian empire included Palestine. In 586, the Judeans refused to pay their tribute (perhaps encouraged by Egyptian promises of support), prompting a Babylonian attack. This resulted in the destruction of Jerusalem and beginning of the Babylonian exile.

The Babylonian empire was relatively short lived. The Persians, subject to the Medes, rebelled. They established a new kingdom, headed by Cyrus the Great, by 550 BCE. They then attacked and conquered Asia Minor (547 BCE) and later Babylon (539 BCE). Cyrus allowed the Judean exiles to return to Jerusalem in the "Edit of Cyrus." Many exiles chose to stay in Babylon, rather than return to their rather insignificant province.

This is summarized in Table 15–1.

TERMINOLOGY

The people to be studied in this section have a variety of different labels applied to them: Israelites, Judeans, and Jews. We cannot use these terms interchangeably, because the Israelites were not Jews (or vice versa). Here are how these terms are defined and should be used:

Israel—The northern kingdom, which extended from just north of Jerusalem to north of the Sea of Galilee

Israelites—In its narrow sense, this term refers only to the people living in the northern kingdom, the kingdom of Israel. This is the way it is usually used in the books of 1 and 2 Kings.

TABLE 15–1

Events in Israel & Judah	Events in Ancient Near East
	2000–1200 Egyptian Domination in Canaan
1200—Israelite settlement in highlands	1250–1150—Invasions of the sea peoples
1200–1000—Judges period	
1000–922—United Kingdom	
922—Split of kingdom into Israel and Judah	900–800—Rise of Assyria
722—Fall of Samaria and Exile of Israelites	By 670 the Assyrian empire included Assyria, Babylonia, Syria, Palestine, and the Egyptian delta. Empire quickly declined after 650
640–609—King Josiah	Babylon revolted against Assyria and became independent in 626. They attacked Assyria and in 612 destroyed Nineveh, Assyria's capital. Established Neo-Babylonian empire
586—Fall of Jerusalem and Exile of Judahites Babylonian exile	
538—Decree of Cyrus ended exile and allowed Judahites to return to Jerusalem	550—Beginning of Persian empire. Persians destroyed Babylonian empire and established empire extending from Iran to Asia Minor
515—Jerusalem Temple rebuilding finished	333—Alexander the Great conquered Palestine
458 (or 398?)—Ezra in Jerusalem	
445—Nehemiah in Jerusalem	

The term is sometimes used collectively by biblical authors to refer to all the descendants of Jacob (who was renamed *Israel* in Gen 32:28), including both northern and southern tribes. This is the way Ezekiel uses it. Ezekiel prophesied a century after the northern kingdom was destroyed in 722 and addressed only southerners, but uses the more inclusive term to refer to the ideal state (which included all 12 tribes).

It is also used to refer to the religious practices of people living in Judah and Israel during the pre-Exilic period (before 586 BCE).

Israelis—Citizens of the modern state of Israel. This term does not refer to people in the Bible.

Judah—The southern kingdom, the region inhabited by members of the tribe of Judah

Judahites—People living in Judah, members of the tribe of Judah

Judea—The territory of Jerusalem during the Hellenistic and Roman periods. Judea grew considerably during this period, especially after the Maccabean revolt in 63 BCE, and eventually, under Herod the Great, included the region around Jerusalem (Judea), territory to its south (Idumaea), territory east of the Jordan River (Perea), and land both west of the Sea of Galilee (Galilee), and east of the Sea of Galilee (Gaulanitis)

Judeans—The people living in Judea or those descended from them, but who lived elsewhere (such as in Babylon or Egypt)

Jew—Where the former terms are geographic, this is a religious term. It can be used to refer to the religion of the Judeans in the post-Exilic period (after 538 BCE). It should not be used to refer to the practices of their pre-Exilic ancestors.

At some point (probably during the Hasmonean period, 135–63 BCE) it became possible for non-Judeans to adopt the religious practices of the Judeans, worshipping their God and observing their customs. In modern parlance, we would say they *converted* to Judaism and became Jews.

FOR FURTHER READING

A. Kirk Grayson, "Mesopotamia, History of: History and Culture of Assyria," *Anchor Bible Dictionary (ABD)* 4: 732–55.

A. Kirk Grayson, "Mesopotamia, History of: History and Culture of Babylonia," *ABD* 4: 755–77.

CHAPTER 16

Joshua

Read Joshua 2, 6–11.

In this chapter, we will:

- Consider the goals of the conquest, according to the Bible
- Consider the thesis of the biblical author
- Examine how archaeological data relates to the Bible

According to the Bible, after wandering in the wilderness for a generation as punishment for doubting God (Num 14), Joshua, Moses' successor, led the Israelites into the Promised Land around 1150 BCE. Archaeologists refer to this as the Late Bronze Age. Interestingly, other ancient sources and archaeological evidence suggest that there were many peoples moving around the eastern Mediterranean at roughly this time.

For much of the Bronze Age, Palestine was controlled by Egypt, which refered to it as the province of Canaan. During the Late Bronze Age, the Canaanite cities were abandoned and new people, the Philistines, took over their territories in the costal plain. What happened to the Canaanites? We will look at one possible explanation in this chapter.

The Conquest

The conquest of the Promised Land (Josh 6–11) was a series of Holy Wars. The laws for Holy War (or *herem*) are found in Deut 20. Read Deut 20 and answer the following questions.

A. What were the Israelites to do when they approached a distant town?

B. What were the Israelites to do to the towns in the land God was giving them?

C. What accounts for the different treatment of the two different sets of towns? How does this fit into Deuteronomy's overall theology and program? (*Hint:* Review the Deuteronomy worksheet (Ch. 13).)

*D. What aspects of this program might be theologically troubling? Why?

Conquest Stories

Jericho

  A. Who devised the plan to capture Jericho?

  B. Did the people follow the plan?

  C. Was the plan successful?

  D. What is the point or moral of the story?

Ai

  A. How would you answer the above questions for the conquest of Ai?

  B. How is this story different?

Hazor

  A. How would you answer the above questions for the conquest of Hazor?

*B. What is the basic theological point the biblical author makes with these battle descriptions?

Native Peoples

A. Do the Israelites observe the rules of Holy War at Jericho?

B. Do they observe them with regard to Gibeon?

*What is the point the biblical author is making with these two examples?

C. Compare Josh 10: 40–43 and 11:16–23 with 13:1–7. What is odd about these sets of verses?

Theme: National Origins, Archaeology and the Conquest

Archaeology in the Holy Land was initially undertaken to prove that biblical stories were true. But archaeological data is hard to interpret. William Dever summarized the data in "Archaeology and the Israelite 'Conquest.'" He makes three main points:

1. There is no significant evidence for Israelites in Egypt.
2. There is no evidence for Israelites on the Sinai Peninsula, and its resources would not have supported a group of 1.5 million people for forty years.
3. Of the 19 sites described in Numbers, Joshua, and Judges as destroyed by the Israelites, only three (Bethel, Lachish, and Hazor) show signs of destruction. The other 16 were either uninhabited or were not destroyed.

In short, archaeological data casts serious doubt on the historical veracity of the conquest as described in Joshua.

The conquest is traditionally dated to around 1150, the end of the Late Bronze period in Canaan. Archaeological evidence suggests that around this time there was an explosion of new settlements in the Judean highlands, where the Bible suggests the Israelites were concentrated. Based on the pottery found at these sites, the inhabitants had no connection to Egypt or to Transjordan. Rather, they seem to have come from the large Canaanite cities found on the costal plain. This is also suggested by the technology they used (terrace farms and plastered cisterns), which shows connections to local Canaanite traditions. In short, this data suggests that the people settling in the central hill country were not foreigners from Egypt but came from local cities. The highland settlements were small and self-sufficient, with little evidence of imported goods. The lack of large structures suggests an egalitarian society.

Most of these sites flourished until the tenth century, when they were abandoned. This corresponds to the period when the Bible suggests the Israelite's government shifted to a monarchy, with urban centers and a hierarchical power structure.

The Conquest in Light of Archaeology

Assume that the archaeologists are correct (see box on previous page) about the origin of the settlers in the highland regions (who became Israelites).

*A. Does Joshua disagree with archaeological data?

*B. Why would the Biblical historian want to present the conquest found in Joshua? *Hint*: reread the material on mythic truth (see Chapter 2) and think about the differences between mythic truth and historical truth (assuming the historical model developed by archaeologists is close to correct *and* was known to the Biblical author).

*C. How might the archaeological evidence address the theologically troubling aspects of these stories?

FOR FURTHER READING

Robert G. Boling, "Joshua, Book of," *Anchor Bible Dictionary (ABD)* 3:1002–15.
William G. Dever, "Archaeology, Syro-Palestinian and Biblical," *ABD* 1:354–67.
William G. Dever, "Archaeology and the Israelite 'Conquest,'" *ABD* 3:535–558.
Niles Peter Lemche, "Israel, History of: Premonarchial Period," *ABD* 3:526–45.

CHAPTER 17

Judges

Read Judges 1–4, 6–8:21, 10–16

In this chapter, we will:

- Learn about redaction criticism
- Study the government of the Judges

The book of Judges describes the period between the Israelites' settlement in Canaan and the monarchy. The nation was led by "judges." We will examine the nature of their leadership in this chapter. We will do this by using another scholarly methodology: redaction criticism.

REDACTION CRITICISM

Like source criticism, redaction criticism assumes that the Bible is composed of different sources. But where source criticism is interested in sorting and dating different sources, redaction criticism is interested in the goals and method of the editor (or *redactor*) who assembled the sources and put them into their present form. We can think about redaction criticism on two different scales: micro and macro.

On the micro scale, a redaction critic looks for the "seams" between different sources, the linking material written by the redactor to connect the disparate sources they had at their disposal. Frequently, "seams" can be identified by similar language used to connect different stories. This is evident in the introductions and conclusions to the reigns of different kings in the books of 1 and 2 Kings:

In the X [number] year of King PN [personal name] of Israel, PN began to reign over Judah; he reigned X years in Jerusalem. . ." (1 Kg 14:21, 15:1, 15:9, etc.)

Now the rest of the deeds of PN, are they not written in the Book of the Chronicles of the Kings of Judah? [or "Kings of Israel"] (1 Kg 14:18, 15:11, 15:21, etc.)

These introductions and conclusions signal that the biblical author had access to books we do not (perhaps royal archives from Judah and Israel). The biblical account abridges these materials, to create a document with a different intent than the originals. If we had access to the original documents, we could do macro-scale redaction criticism.

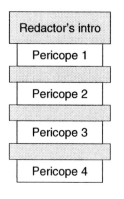

Figure 17–1. Redaction Criticism. Stories (or pericopes) are created and circulate independently. At some point, they are together by a redactor (or editor). The shaded blocks in the diagram represent the text supplied by the redactor to connect the stories. A redaction critic studies the connective material (the shaded blocks) to try to discern the editor's thesis, goal, or bias.

Macro-scale redaction criticism examines the revisional activity for a whole book. Ideally, we would have both the sources the redactor used and the finished product, so we could see exactly what changes the redactor made to their source(s). By doing this comparison, we would be able to guess why the redactor made the changes.

Unfortunately, there is only one place in the Hebrew Bible where this happy situation is found. The books of Chronicles revise large portions of 2 Samuel, and 1 and 2 Kings to produce an alternate history. We will do macro-scale redaction criticism when we study Chronicles (Chapter 25).

We will do micro-scale redaction criticism on Table 17–1. Fill out this chart as you read through Judges 1–4, 6–8:21, 11–16.

TABLE 17–1

Judge	Length of Reign	Who is Oppressed?	Who is the Oppressor?	Which Tribes Fight?[1]
Othniel	40 years (3:11)	Israelites (3:11)	None specified	None specified
Ehud				3:27
Deborah				4:6
Gideon/Jerubbaal				6:35
Jephthah				11:5–6,11
Samson				

Remember, our goal in micro-scale redaction criticism is to look for "seams." As with 1 and 2 Kings, it would be natural to look for seams at the beginning and end of the reigns of different judges.

[1]For names of the various tribes, see p. 26.

Study Table 17–1 and answer the following questions:

A. What is unusual or unexpected about the length the judges reign?

B. Look at columns three (who is oppressed) and five (which tribes fight). What is odd about them?

*C. What materials in Judges do you think could be attributed to a redactor?

Older Sources

It is sometimes possible to say something about the sources used by a redactor, even if we do not have them at our disposal. It may be possible to do this with the materials used by the redactor of Judges.

Locate the tribes who respond to the different judges on Map 5–1 (see p. 26).

A. Where are Ehud, Deborah, and Gideon active?

B. How about Jephthah?

C. How about Samson?

*D. What do each set of sources have in common geographically?

Government

A. How many tribes did most Judges seem to control?

B. How united were the Israelites (see Jdg 8:1–3, 12:1–6)?

Judges' Characters

Judges offers a delightful collection of stories, exhibiting, again, the characteristic traits of Hebrew narrative. We will only briefly examine two of them.

Ehud (3:12–30)

A. What unusual fact about Ehud is highlighted when he is first introduced?

B. What is described in unexpected detail? Why are these two points significant to the story?

C. Ehud says two things to the king. How are they different? How are these differences significant?

D. A humorous (?) note might be suggested by where Ehud delivered God's "message" to Eglon. Read vss. 24–25. Why did Eglon's servants not realize immediately he was dead?

Theme: Women

Judges is interesting for the number of strong female characters found in it. They include the prophetess/judge Deborah and Jael, killer of Sisera. One unfamiliar character may be Jephthah's daughter.

Reread Genesis 22, the binding of Isaac, and then read Jdg 11:29–40.

A. Why did Abraham plan to sacrifice Isaac?

B. Why did Jephthah sacrifice his daughter?

C. How does the Biblical author describe Jephthah's realization that he will have to kill his daughter?

D. What was the attitude of the victims in each story to the plan?

E. How do the stories end differently?

Figure 17–2. Gustave Doré, a nineteenth century French artist, produced illustrations for many famous texts, including the Bible. His work is characterized by dramatic poses and strong contrasts between light and dark. It was criticized by his contemporaries as being too theatrical. Perhaps for this reason, it influenced 20th century film makers, especially Cecil B. DeMille.[2] Doré's drawing of Jael's killing of Sisera demonstrates these traits.

Deborah and Barak (4:1–24)

A. How is Deborah introduced?

B. We saw above (see Chapter 7) that the first words uttered by a character may be especially significant in describing their character. What do we learn about Barak?

[2]Millicent Rose, *The Doré Bible Illustrations* (New York: Dover Publications, Inc., 1974).

C. How is this impression reinforced by Deborah's subsequent utterances?

D. How does Deborah's prediction (vs. 9) come to pass?

FOR FURTHER READING

Robert G. Boling, "Judges, Book of," *Anchor Bible Dictionary (ABD)* 3:1107–1116.
John Barton, "Redaction Criticism: Old Testament," *ABD* 5:644–47.
Niles Peter Lemche, "Israel, History of: Premonarchial Period," *ABD* 3:526–45.

CHAPTER 18

Early Monarchy

Read Judges 8:21–9:57, 17–21; 1 Sam 1–2, 7–12.

In this chapter, we will:

- Consider the arguments against a monarchy
- Consider what happens when there is no monarchy
- Think about who *should* be Israel's king

The end of the Bronze Age saw dramatic changes in the balance of power in the eastern Mediterranean. One of the most significant was the decline in the power of Egypt, which controlled Palestine for much of the Bronze Age. The resulting power vacuum saw the emergence of many different "nations," including the Philistines and Phoenicians (along Palestine's coastal plain), and the Israelites, Ammonites, Moabites, and several other inland states.

Each of these different nations attempted to dominate its neighbors. The Philistines attempted to expand inland and attacked the Israelites. This is often seen as the reason the Israelites abandoned the system described in Judges. There were two main problems with the Judges system. First, there was no strong central government that could support a standing army and resist well organized outside attacks. Second, when a judge died, there was no clear successor to assume control of the government. Both these problems can be observed in the first part of Judges. Having a monarchy would solve both these problems, but, as we will see, the transition to monarchy was difficult and took several generations.

Later authors, including those living under a king, sometimes questioned whether it was the best form of government. This chapter will look at the movement towards a monarchy and the various responses to having a king.

Attitude about Monarchy in Judges

Jdg 8:22–9:57

A. What is Gideon's response to the request that he become king?

B. Gideon's *ephod* may have been designed to allow God "to rule over" the Israelites. Does the biblical author think it worked?

Gideon's son, Abimelech (whose name means "my father [is] king") established a monarchy.

C. What did he do to his brothers? (His actions, as we will see, are not unusual in monarchies)

D. What is the point of Jotham's "Parable of the Trees"?

Abimelech's reign was short, only three years.

E. What caused his relations to sour with Shechem?

F. Is Jotham's curse fulfilled?

Jdg 17–21

*ZRead the last four chapters in Judges closely. It is a collection of several stories, united by a common theme describing life during the (end?) of the Judges era.

A. What do Jdg 17:6, 18:1, 19:1, and 21:25 have in common? What is the attitude in this section of Judges towards a monarchy?

The Levite's Concubine (Jdg 19)

This story is one of the most disturbing in the Bible. It may be compared to the story about Sodom (Gen 19). You may want to read both together and consider them as a type-scene (see Chapter 7).

  A. Why does the Levite pass by Jebus?

  B. Who does the old man offer to the crowd?

  C. Is the concubine dead when the Levite dismembers her?

Judges 20–21

  A. What is the response to the Levite's gruesome message?

  B. How are the Benjamites saved from dying out?

*Reading these four chapters, how did the people act when they "did what was right in their own eyes"?

*How does this relate to the institution of the monarchy?

Cutting Covenants?

When Saul hears that Nahash, the Ammonite king, was attacking the Israelites at Jabesh-gilead, he took two oxen and "cut them in pieces and sent them throughout all the territories of Israel by messengers, saying, 'Whoever does not come out after Saul and Samuel, so shall it be done to his oxen'" (1 Sam 11:7). This story recalls that of the Levite's concubine, in which the Levite chopped up his concubine, and sent her pieces throughout the tribes. In both cases, the response was that the tribes mustered and went to war.

What is the origin of this odd custom?

When the Israelites made an agreement, they described it as *cutting* a covenant. It is possible that this was not just a figure of speech, but that cutting animals was part of the covenant ceremony. In Gen 15:7–21, God made a covenant with Abram, who cut a heifer, a goat, and a ram in half. In a dream, he saw a smoking pot and a torch pass between the pieces of animal.

Dismembering an animal thus may have served to recall the covenant binding the tribes together. It may have also been a threat: as Saul said, "Whoever does not come out . . . so shall it be done to his oxen."

Monarchy in 1 Samuel

Samuel is a prophet *and* the last judge, the man who annoints the first king, Saul.

A. Read 1 Sam 7. What themes connect this chapter with the themes in Judges?

B. Pay special attention to 7:15–17. This sounds historically plausible: Samuel goes from religious site to site, administering justice. What sites are mentioned?

1 Sam 8

A. Who does Samuel think should be Israel's king?

B. What will a king do?

Saul

Saul was the first king in Israel, but the stories about him are oddly conflicted.

1 Sam 9:1–2

A. How is Saul introduced? (Remember, details are significant in biblical narrative.)

1 Sam 9:27–10:16

A. What does Samuel do to Saul here? What does Saul tell him?

B. How does this compare to Samuel's comments in 1 Sam 8?

1 Sam 10:17–27

A. Are Samuel's comments here more akin to those of 1 Sam 8 or 1 Sam 9?

B. How is Saul described here? How does it differ from 1 Sam 9?

Analysis

Notice that the Biblical authors' attitude towards the monarchy is conflicted.

A. Where is the monarchy seen as a good thing?

B. Where is it seen as a bad thing?

C. Who would like a monarchy?

D. Who would dislike it?

FOR FURTHER READING

Walter Brueggemann, "Samuel, Book of 1–2: Narrative and Theology," *Anchor Bible Dictionary (ABD)* 5:965–73.

Leslie J. Hoppe, "Israel, History of: Monarchic Period," *ABD* 3:558–67.

Keith W. Whitelam, "King and Kingship," *ABD* 4:40–48.

Diana V. Edelman, "Saul," *ABD* 5:989–999.

George W. Ramsey, "Samuel," *ABD* 5:954–57.

CHAPTER 19

King Saul and David

Read 1 Sam 13–19, 22:1–5, 24–25, 28, 30–31, 2 Sam 1–2:10, 5:5.

In this chapter, we will:

- Use historical methodology to study the reigns of David and Saul
- Think about the biblical historian's goal and bias

David replaced Saul as king. This was unusual, since a king was usually succeeded by his son. How and why did this happen? The Biblical author presents one explanation of why this happened and data to support it. We will examine the data closely and see if we can formulate an alternative hypothesis, one that might be more persuasive to a modern historian.

1 Sam 13:1, 14:47–52

A. How successful is Saul as king?

The Biblical Author's Explanation of Why Saul's Dynasty Didn't Continue

A. Saul makes three mistakes in 1 Sam 13–15. List them:

1.

2.

3.

B. What is God's response to Saul's mistakes?

A Historical-Critical Analysis of the Shift from Saul to David

Read 1 Sam 13–19, 24 and answer the following questions.

Biblical Explanation for Saul's Fear and Persecution of David

A. What initially prompted Saul to begin to fear David?

B. Why did Saul want David to marry his daughter Michal?

C. Why do you think the DH so carefully reports the affection felt by Jonathan and Michal towards David?

D. What does the story in Chapter 24 suggest about David's attitude toward Saul?

E. Why did David depart from Saul's service?

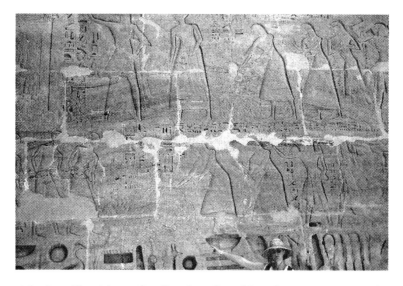

Figure 19–1. The idea of collecting foreskins from your enemies seems distasteful to modern readers, but Saul was not the only king to request them. This Egyptian relief shows Pharoah's servants bringing foreskins and piling them before him (where the woman is pointing).

A. Who joined David when he was in flight from Saul (22:1–2)?

B. What were David and his men doing in Chapter 25? (Imagine Don Corleone or Tony Soprano saying the words in 25:6–8!)

C. Why did David want to marry Abigail? (*Hint:* what is the first thing the Bible says about Nabal, her husband?)

D. What did David do with the spoils from Ziklag (30:26–31)?

Analysis

*A. Does the DH think Saul's fear of David was rational?

*B. Does the data suggest that Saul's fear of David *was* rational?

*C. According to the Bible, David went to Hebron and was elected king *after* Saul's death (2 Sam 2:1–4). At the same time, Abner, Saul's general, took Ishbaal, Saul's son, and made him king (2 Sam 2:8–10). Look at the length of Ishbaal's reign (2 Sam 2:10) and David's reign over Judah (2 Sam 5:5).

1. Assuming the text is correct (that is, without scribal errors), what is the problem with these dates?

2. Can you think of an explanation for the discrepancy?

FOR FURTHER READING

Walter Brueggemann, "Samuel, Book of 1–2: Narrative and Theology," *Anchor Bible Dictionary* (*ABD*) 5:965–73.

Leslie J. Hoppe, "Israel, History of: Monarchic Period," *ABD* 3:558–67.

Keith W. Whitelam, "King and Kingship," *ABD* 4:40–48.

Diana V. Edelman, "Saul," *ABD* 5:989–999.

David M. Howard, Jr., "David," *ABD* 2:41–49.

CHAPTER 20

David's Monarchy

Read 2 Sam 1–7, 9, 11–19, 21.

In this chapter, we will:

- Think about how David became king
- Study how David governed his kingdom

David did not immediately assume the throne when Saul died. In this worksheet, we will look at *how* David came to be king, first of Judah, and later of Israel. The Biblical author briefly notes David's positive accomplishments before giving a long, protracted description of the problems in David's house. Again, we will look at these data and note the Biblical author's explanation for David's rise and fall and see if we can think of an alternative scenario that might be more persuasive to a modern historian.

David's Campaign: Read 2 Sam 1–5:5

A. What did David do to the messenger who reports Saul's death?

B. What did he do to Baanah and Rechab, the killers of Ishbaal?

C. What did he do after he heard of the death of Saul?

D. What did he do after he heard about the death of Abner?

E. According to the biblical author, why did David respond in this manner, when the deaths of Saul, Abner, and Ishbaal benefit him enormously?

F. What other explanations can you think of for David's behavior?

The End of Saul's Dynasty

A. What happened to Saul and Jonathan (1 Sam 31, 2 Sam 1)?

B. What happened to Saul's other sons (2 Sam 21)?[1]

C. What is Mephiboshet's initial reaction to David's invitation? Why does he react this way? Why might David want him in Jerusalem? (2 Sam 9)

D. Do you think David upheld his vow to Saul (1 Sam 24:20)?

David's Kingdom

Type of Monarchy

A. Review 1 Sam 10:25. When Saul becomes king, what does Samuel do?

B. Read 2 Sam 2:4. Who makes David king?

C. Read 2 Sam 5:3. Who makes David king? How does this parallel Saul's ascent to the throne?

*D. Were either David or Saul absolute monarchs?

David was a savvy politician and realized that he could not rule Israel from Hebron, the city where he was crowned. Rather, he sought a neutral city, between Israel and Judah, and found it in Jebus. Read 2 Sam 5:6–6:23.

---

[1]Most scholars think that 2 Sam 21 is misplaced due to a scribal error. The text makes more sense if it was located between chapters 8 and 9. For more information, see P. K. McCarter, Jr., *Anchor Bible 9: 2 Samuel* (Garden City, NY: Doubleday, 1984).

A. What happens to Jebus? Note its two names (5:6 and 5:9).

B. What does he move there? Why would he want to do this?

For later biblical authors, the fact that David's dynasty continued for about four centuries was miraculous. It is explained in Nathan's Oracle. Read 1 Sam 7.

A. What does "house" mean in this chapter?

B. What does God's covenant promise David?

This oracle inspired some prophets to predict the restoration of David's house after Jerusalem's destruction. When the expected restoration did not happen, later Jews projected their expectation into the future—a messiah would arise from David's lineage. As we will see, the writers of the gospels claimed this expectation was fulfilled in Jesus.

David's Descent

You may have noticed a parallel structure to the reigns of Saul and David. They follow a "poor boy done good" pattern. Each starts out modestly, struggles against opponents, becomes king, and then their reign falls apart, descending into chaos. This pattern is especially apparent in the life of David.

A. Chapters 13–20 record at least three major disasters for David and his family. List them:

1.

2.

3.

The Promised Land

David took advantage of the power vacuum arising from the weakness of Egypt and the Mesopotamian civilizations to establish a large empire. He controlled more land than any other Israelite king. Possibly for this reason, he was regarded by the biblical author(s) as the king most blessed by God.

The boundaries of his empire are described in 2 Sam 8:1–14. If you compare these boundaries with those of the land promised to Abram (see Chapter 6), you will notice they are quite similar. It is for this reason that many scholars believe that the stories about Abram were collected, edited, and "published" during the time of the united monarchy.

After the united monarchy ended (with Solomon's death) and the kingdom divided, the empire quickly fell apart and most subject peoples gained their independence, as we will see in 1 and 2 Kings.

Figure 20–1. Doré depicts the instant before Absalom's death, with Joab and his excited men rushing into darkness to finish off the rebel.

B. According to the biblical historian, what caused these problems? (See Chapter 12.)

C. How does Absalom gain adherents for his revolt (Chapter 15)?

D. Once Absalom's revolt is suppressed, how does David gain control over Judah (Chapter 19)?

E. How does he gain control over Israel (Chapter 20)?

F. What do the revolts of Absalom and Sheba suggest about David's popularity?

Something to Think About: Joab

Joab is David's general and seems a very bloodthirsty character. He killed lots of people, but two are singled out for special notice: Abner and Amasa (1 Kg 2:5). It is implied that David did not desire their deaths (2 Sam 3:28–29). Is Joab a psychopath or can his killings be explained rationally? Consider the following questions:

What is the position of Abner in Saul and Ishbaal's kingdom? What do you think David promised him to gain his support (2 Sam 3: 12–21)?

What is the position of Amasa in Absalom's army (17:25)? What do you think David promised him to gain his support (2 Sam 19:13–15)?

Why would Joab kill these men? Do you think David was surprised by these killings? Do you think David did not want them killed?

Analysis

David's Rise

   A. How does the Biblical historian explain David's rise to king?

   B. How would a modern historian explain his rise?

David's Fall

   A. How does the Biblical historian explain the problems in David's house?

   B. How would a modern historian explain David's problems?

FOR FURTHER READING

Walter Brueggemann, "Samuel, Book of 1–2: Narrative and Theology," *Anchor Bible Dictionary* (*ABD*) 5:965–73.

Leslie J. Hoppe, "Israel, History of: Monarchic Period," *ABD* 3:558–67.

Keith W. Whitelam, "King and Kingship," *ABD* 4:40–48.

David M. Howard, Jr., "David," *ABD* 2:41–49.

D. G. Schley, "Joab," *ABD* 3:852–54.

CHAPTER 21

Solomon

Read 1 Kg 1–2, 4–7:1, 9, 11.

In this chapter, we will:

- Compare the way David and Solomon ruled
- Study the changing role of the monarchy

Solomon's monarchy was *very* different than his father's. We will see that the way Solomon became king was nothing like David's ascent. Solomon's government and accomplishments were also very different.

Solomon's Ascent to the Throne

David's Sons

Read 2 Sam 3:2–5 and fill in column 2 with the names of David's male offspring. Then review your notes (or reread 2 Sam 13–18) and complete column 3.

TABLE 21–1

Son #	Name of Son	What Happened to Him?
1		
2	Chileab	Never mentioned again. Died in infancy?
3		
4		
?	?	First child of Bathsheba died in infancy (2 Sam 12:15b–18)
?	Solomon	

Solomon's Supporters

1 Kg 1 describes how Solomon became king instead of his rival Adonijah. Each had his supporters. Read the chapter and fill in Table 21–2.

TABLE 21–2

Government Faction	Support Adonijah	Support Solomon
Military		
Priestly		
Prophetic		

"David's own warriors" (v. 8b) are probably his palace guard, an elite military unit.

1 Kg 1:11–37

A. How would you characterize David's mental acuity?

B. Briefly outline the plot to enthrone Solomon—who are the major actors and what steps to they take to achieve their goal?

C. Do you believe David promised Bathsheba that Solomon would succeed him? Why or why not?

Solomon's Opponents

After he became king, what happened to Solomon's opponents (listed in column 2 of Table 21–2)? Answer the following questions to answer this question.

1 Kg 2:13–25

In ancient Israel, one way a usurper could demonstrate his control of the kingdom was to take possession of the king's harem. David left some concubines in Jerusalem when he fled (2 Sam 15:16) and Absalom had intercourse with them (2 Sam 16:20–21). The same custom is mentioned in 2 Sam 3:7, with Ishbaal and Abner.

A. Why might one suspect this is Solomonic propaganda? List at least two reasons:

1.

2.

1 Kg 2:5-6

A. Do you think this is Solomonic propaganda? How about 2:28–35?

1 Kg 2:26-27

A. This is the only opponent of Solomon who lives. Why do you think Solomon didn't order his execution? Note that this left the Temple with only one priest, Zadok (or his son), a southerner.

Solomon's Government

Solomon's government was quite different from that of David, as is evident from Table 21–3.

TABLE 21–3

Office	David (2 Sam 8:15–18)	Solomon (1 Kg 4:1–7)
General		
Recorder		
Priests		
Secretary		
Other		
		Adoniram – Forced labor

Solomon's government is larger than David's government.

A. What goes along with bigger governments? (*Hint:* look at 1 Kg 4:22 and 27.)

1 Kg 4:7-19

This passage describes a reorganization of Solomon's government. Look at the map of his administrative districts on p. 104 and compare it to map of the tribal boundaries (p. 26).

A. What was Solomon trying to accomplish with this reorganization? (*Hint:* see 4:26–28.)

B. How do you think the regions were administered under David? (*Hint:* review Chapter 20 on David's monarchy.)

C. What regional bias can you discern in this organization?

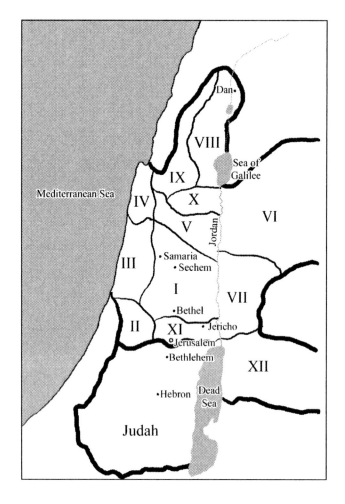

Map 21–1. This map shows approximately where Solomon's administrative districts were located.

Solomon's Construction Projects

1 Kg 6

A. What are the dimensions of the temple Solomon built?

B. How long did it take to build?

1 Kg 7:1–12

C. What are the dimensions of Solomon's Palace?

D. How long did it take to build?

E. Why do you think the Biblical author so closely juxtaposed the time spent on the temple with that spent on the palace? (See 6:38, 7:1.)

1 Kg 5, 9:10–11, 15–22

F. How did Solomon pay for the construction of the temple?

G. What regional bias does he display here?

God's Promises

A. Recall the covenant God made with David (2 Sam 7). God makes two similar promises with Solomon (1 Kg 6:11–13, 9:1–9). Pay special attention to the second (longer) promise. How is it similar or different from the covenant with David?

FOR FURTHER READING

Steven W. Holloway, "Kings, Book of 1–2," *Anchor Bible Dictionary (ABD)* 4:69–83.
Leslie J. Hoppe, "Israel, History of: Monarchic Period," *ABD* 3:558–67.
Keith W. Whitelam, "King and Kingship," *ABD* 4:40–48.
Tomoo Ishida, "Solomon," *ABD* 6:105–13.

CHAPTER 22

Kings of Israel (Northern Kingdom)

In this chapter, we will:

- Study the dynastic patterns in the northern kingdom of Israel
- Compare the biblical historian's explanation of why Israel and Judah split apart with that of modern historians.

As mentioned in Chapter 19, David took advantage of a power vacuum to create a regional empire. The "superpowers" remained weak during the reign of Solomon, but beginning in the 9th century, the Assyrians, located in the northern part of Mesopotamia, began to expand and eventually established control over all of Palestine and even, briefly, Egypt.

It is doubtful that Israel and Judah, united, could have withstood the Assyrians, but David's kingdoms split in 922, when Solomon died. The other regions in David's empire (Aram, Edom, Moab, Ammon) also split off and regained their independence. As in the period before Saul and David, all these states fought amongst themselves, seeking advantage over their neighbors. The history of these interactions are exceedingly complex and we will not dwell on them.

Rather, we will think about several issues of greater concern for the biblical authors: Why did the kingdom split? Why was Israel exiled?

As with the previous sheets, we will think about the explanation the biblical author offers for these disasters and consider alternatives that might be more plausible to a modern historian. We will also think about the goal and audience of the biblical author.

Skim through 1 and 2 Kings, reading the passages in the "citation" column of this table and completing the fourth and fifth columns. Pay special attention to the "Evaluation" column—what do the kings do that is good or bad?

Draw a line between the names of the kings when a dynasty changes—that is, when someone other than the son of the king becomes king.

TABLE 22–1

Citation	Name	Length of Reign	Pre-King Occupation	Evaluation of the King by Biblical Historian
1 Kg 11:26–40, 12:2–3, 12:25–14:20	Jeroboam I	22 yrs		
15:25–26	Nadab	2 yrs		
15:27–16:7	Baasha	24 yrs		
16:6–10	Elah	2 yrs		
16:9–20	Zimri	7 days		
16:16–28	Omri	12 yrs		
16:29, 22:39–40	Ahab	22 yrs		
22:51–53, 2 Kg 1:17–18	Ahaziah	2 yrs		
3:1–3, 9:14–26	Jehoram (or Joram)	12 yrs		
9:1–13, 10:1–36	Jehu	28 yrs		
13:1–9	Jehoahaz	17 yrs		
14:8–16	Jehoash	16 yrs		
14:23–27	Jeroboam II	41 yrs		
15:8–9	Zechariah	6 mo.		
15:10–13	Shallum	1 mo.		
15:13–22	Menahem	10 yrs		
15:23–26	Pekahiah	2 yrs		
15:27–31	Pekah	20 yrs		
17:1–6	Hoshea	9 yrs		

Analysis of Table 22–1

A. Look at the fourth column. What are the two ways people became kings in Israel?

*B. Look at the last column. What are the criteria the biblical historian uses to evaluate the kings?

C. What other criteria can you think of to judge whether a king is "good" or "bad"?

Why Did Kingdoms Split?

1 Kg 11–13

A. According to the biblical historian, why did Israel split away from Rehoboam? (*Hint:* review ch 11.)

B. Review the Solomon worksheet. List at least two mundane, *political* reasons that the Northern tribes might have had to reject Rehoboam's rule:

 1.

 2.

C. When did the Northern tribes revolt previously? Against which king?

*D. How did the biblical historian explain the splitting of the kingdom in light of God's eternal covenant with David (2 Sam 7) that his house (or children) would always remain enthroned over Israel? (*Hint:* see 1 Kg 9 and 11.)

Intended Audience for the History

A. List at least four elements of Jeroboam's cultic reform (1 Kg 12:25–33):

 1.

 2.

 3.

 4.

*B. Why do you think the biblical author condemns Jeroboam's bulls as "idols" but does not label the cherubim in the Jerusalem temple (1 Kg 6:23–28) in the same way?

Figure 22–1. Here are images of two statues, one of Shiva and one of Jesus. Is either of these statues an "idol"? What makes one an "idol" and the other not an "idol"?

2 Kg 17:7–23

*C. List at least six activities the biblical author condemns.

　　1.

　　2.

　　3.

　　4.

　　5.

　　6.

*D. How many of these items can you find in the last column of Table 22–1? How many were part of Jeroboam's cultic reforms (p. 109)?

D. How does God punish Israel in 2 Kg 17?

Analysis

A. Since this description is written after the destruction and exile of the northern tribes, who is its audience?

B. Since the reasons for the exile (2 Kg 17, see p. 110) are not the same as the sins of Jeroboam or Israel, who was doing the things condemned in this list?

Theophoric Names

Students find many names from the Hebrew Bible confusing because "they all sound the same." This similarity arises from the fact that many biblical names contain the Hebrew words for either "god" (*el*) or part of the divine name (*jah* or *je* or *iah* are all shortened versions of Yah / Yahweh). These are often used in combination with other nouns, such as *ah* ("brother") or *ab* ("father"), or verbs. Frequently these names can be translated as simple sentences.

Elijah = Eli + jah = "my God (is) Yahweh" (1 Kg 17:1)
Ahijah = Ahi + jah = "my brother (is) Yahweh" (1 Kg 11:29)
Abijah = Abi + jah = "my father (is) Yahweh" (1 Kg 14:1)
Elisha = Eli + sha = "my God (is) salvation" (1 Kg 19:16)
Obadiah = Obad + iah = "servant of Yahweh" (1 Kg 18:3)
Shemaiah = Shema + iah = "heard by Yahweh" (1 Kg 12:22)
Micah (or Micaiah) = Mi + ca + iah = "Who (is) like Yahweh" (1 Kg 22:8)
Zedekiah = Zedek + iah = "righteous (is) Yahweh" (1 Kg 22:11)
Amaziah = Amaz + iah = "Mighty (is) Yahweh" (2 Kg 13:12)
Zechariah = Zechar + iah = "Yahweh has helped" (2 Kg 15:8)
Jehu = Je + hu = "Yahweh (is) He" (1 Kg 16:1)
Jehoshaphat = Jeh + shaphat = "Yahweh has judged" (1 Kg 22:2)
Jehoram or Joram = Jeh + ram = "Yahweh is exalted" (2 Kg 1:17)

The technical term for personal names that incorporate elements of the divine name is *theophoric*, meaning "bearing or containing the name of a god." This comes from the Greek: *theos* (god) + *phoroiai* (carry or bear).

FOR FURTHER READING

Steven W. Holloway, "Kings, Book of 1–2," *Anchor Bible Dictionary (ABD)* 4:69–83.

Leslie J. Hoppe, "Israel, History of: Monarchic Period," *ABD* 3:558–67.

Carl D. Evans, "Jeroboam," *ABD* 3:742–45.

CHAPTER 23

Kings of Judah (Southern Kingdom)

In this chapter, we will:

- Study the dynastic patterns in the southern kingdom of Judah
- Contrast how the biblical historian thought Judah *should* worship and how they *did* worship
- Examine the way the biblical historian explains why Judah went into exile

A table of the Judean kings is much less interesting than that of the northern kings. With one exception (Queen Athalia, 1 Kg 11:1–20), they are all descendants of David. They are judged by the same criteria as the kings of Israel. The main difference is that some Judean kings are rated positively by the biblical historian. Hence, we will focus our attention on the best and worst of the Judean kings.

Rehoboam

1 Kg 12:1–19, 14:21–31

A. Like Jeroboam in Israel, Rehoboam introduced (or tolerated or reintroduced?) worship practices that the biblical author thought illicit in Judah. List at least three of these:

1.

2.

3.

B. What sorts of relations were there between Israel and Judah?

C. How strong was Judah in international politics?

Ahaz

2 Kg 16

A. What prompted Ahaz to contact Tiglath-Pilesar?

B. How did he persuade Tiglath-Pilesar to assist him?

C. Ahaz became an Assyrian vassal, with Tiglath-Pilesar his suzerain lord. Vassals typically had to pay their suzerain tribute, and to honor them, sometimes by offering sacrifices on their behalf. Why might we suspect that Ahaz was required to do this?

Reforms of Hezekiah and Josiah

Hezekiah reigned from 715 to 687 BCE, during the final phase of Assyria's expansion. Assyria began to weaken dramatically after 650, opposed by Egypt and Babylon. Josiah took advantage of this and expanded his kingdom into the north (he visited, for example, Bethel, 2 Kg 23:15–20). But at the end of his life, Josiah got caught between the major powers, as he tried to help the Babylonians by attacking Pharaoh Neco, a fatal mistake.

Read 2 Kg 18, 22–23 carefully and fill out Table 23–1 (some squares may be blank).

TABLE 23–1

	Hezekiah (2 Kg 18:1–12)	Josiah (2 Kings 22–23)
1. What prompted king to start reform program?		
2. What changes were made to the temple?		
3. What changes were implemented in outside Jerusalem?		
4. Attitude toward God's commandments?		
5. Foreign policy of king?		

A. The biblical historian enthusiastically endorses the reforms of Hezekiah and Josiah. Do you think would have been popular at the time? Why or why not?

B. What evidence can you find in the biblical accounts that they were popular? (*Hint:* look at the response to Josiah's reading of the law and his Passover, both in Chapter 23. Do you think these are trustworthy?)

C. What evidence can you find that they were unpopular? (*Hint:* look at the speech of the Rabshakeh (2 Kg 18:19–26) and the priestly response to Josiah, 23:4–9. Do you think these are trustworthy?)

Figure 23–1. The Bible makes it clear that there were many local cult sites in ancient Judah. This photo shows the cult site in Arad. On the left is the holy of holies (where the deity "resided"). The courtyard in front contained a square altar.

Exile of Judah

2 Kg 21:1–17, 24–25

The Babylonians took over much of the former Assyrian empire and Judah fell under their dominion after Josiah's death (2 Kg 24:1). They took the Judahites into exile in two waves, the first in 597 BCE, and the second with the destruction of Jerusalem in 586.

A. Who does the biblical historian blame for the exile of the Judahites?

B. How is this explained in light of the covenants with David and Solomon (see chapter 22)?

C. The biblical historian assessed the last few Judean kings negatively (chapters 24–25). What, exactly, did they do that was bad?

D. How do their evil deeds compare with earlier kings (i.e., Rehoboam or Ahaz)?

E. Who did the Babylonians take into exile? Who did they leave behind? What was their strategy in who they took and who they left?

··

FOR FURTHER READING

Steven W. Holloway, "Kings, Book of 1–2," *Anchor Bible Dictionary* (*ABD*) 4:69–83.
Leslie J. Hoppe, "Israel, History of: Monarchic Period," *ABD* 3:558–67.
Keith W. Whitelam, "Ahaz," *ABD* 1:106–07.
Jonathan Rosenbaum, "Hezekiah King of Judah," *ABD* 3:189–193.
Robert Althann, "Josiah," *ABD* 3:1015–18.

CHAPTER 24

Deuteronomistic History

In this chapter, we will:

- Pull together common themes and ideas from the books of Joshua through Second Kings
- Outline and evaluate the scholarly thesis about the Deuteronomistic History

Many scholars call the books of Joshua, Judges, Samuel and Kings the Deuteronomistic History. By reviewing several worksheets, we will try to judge whether this label is appropriate or not.

Why Call It the *"Deuteronomistic History"*?

Review the Deuteronomy worksheet (Chapter 13).

A. What did Deuteronomy fear the Israelites would do when they entered the land?

B. What did God promise to do if the Israelites disobeyed?

C. Review Deut 12. How were the native peoples worshipping? How and where were Israelites (and Judahites) supposed to worship?

D. Review the Joshua worksheet (Chapter 16). What is the basic thesis of the author of this text?

E. Review the Judges worksheet (Chapter 17). What is the main thesis of the book of Judges?

F. Review the Northern Kings worksheet (Chapter 22). Who was the worst king? Why?

G. Review the Southern Kings worksheet (Chapter 23). Who was a good king? Why?

*H. What is the common theme between Deut 28, Judges, and why the Israelites went into exile?

*I. Do you think there are enough similarities between the books of Deut, Josh, Judges, Samuel, and Kings to posit a common editor/author/redactor? Why or why not?

Date and Authorship

Most scholars think the DH went through two editions. Answer the following questions to identify the author/date of the first edition:

A. Review 1 Kg 13:1–6. What did the "man of God" predict?

B. Does this come to pass? (*Hint:* answer the next question before this one.)

C. Review 2 Kg 22–23. It has been suggested that the book of the law found by Hilkiah was the book of Deuteronomy. What evidence can you find to support this notion? (*Hint:* Compare Deut 12 and 2 Kg 23.)

Review your Southern Kings worksheet (Chapter 23).

D. What did a king do to get a negative evaluation?

E. What did a king do to get a positive evaluation?

F. Who was the best king?

*Based on your answers to items B and F, when or under whose sponsorship might the DH have been written?

The Second Edition of the DH

Since the book of 2 Kgs doesn't end with the reign of the aforementioned king, someone else must have supplemented it. This may be established by noting the following:

A. Review (again) your Southern Kings worksheet (and the appropriate biblical passages). What is different about the description of the evils of Ahaz and those of the last four kings of Judah?

B. Who is to blame for the exile of Judah? (*Hint:* look at 21:10–15.)

C. What is different about his deeds and those of Ahaz?

D. Might the differences suggest the material about Manasseh is an addition to earlier material?

The date of the supplement cannot be established precisely, but is obviously after the exile of the Judahites (see 2 Kg 25:21, 27–30).

....

FOR FURTHER READING

Steven L. McKenzie, "Deuteronomistic History," *Anchor Bible Dictionary* (*ABD*) 2:160–68.

CHAPTER 25

Chronicles

In this chapter, we will:

- Revisit the method of redaction criticism
- Use redaction criticism to examine the books of Chronicles to figure out the author's thesis or bias

Chronicles is the best example of where redaction criticism (see page 80) can be applied in the Hebrew Bible. We will see that there is good reason to think that the author of the Chronicler's History (CH) had access to the DH, so we can compare both the source (the DH) and the edited product (the CH), and see what the Chronicler tried to accomplish with their revision.

Saul

Read 1 Sam 31, 2 Sam 1:1–16, 2:1–11 and review the David worksheet (Chapter 20).

A. How did Saul die, according to the Deuteronomistic historian (DH)?

B. What happened to Saul's house?

We noted earlier (Chapter 23) that the Babylonians took only a portion of Jerusalem's population into exile (see 2 Kg 24:14–17, 25:11–12), among them the intellectual and religious elite. Some of these people were responsible for the Deuteronomic history (since it was updated, in a second edition, during the exile; see Chapter 24). It is impossible to know for certain how influential the DH school was, but note that 2 Kg 24–25 does not suggest that Josiah's reforms were undone. Does this mean they were embraced by the population? Or does it mean that the editor who finished 2 Kings did not want to report that the reforms were rolled back after Josiah's death?

Assuming that Judah's elite accepted Deuteronomic-type ideology, the exile posed a special problem. If you can only offer sacrifices and worship God in Jerusalem, how could God be worshipped in Babylon? The exiles redefined worship, emphasizing reading and study of scripture (Neh 8) and obeying it (Ezra 7:25–26). They continued practices from the Jerusalem temple that did not involve animal sacrifice: praying and singing psalms. In short, they developed a transportable religion, one that could be practiced anywhere. It is probable that the exiles gathered together to worship. This may be the origin of the synagogue, although it is uncertain.

This was a remarkable innovation in Western religious history. Before this most deities were local deities and were not easily transportable. When one went somewhere new, one worshipped the land's local deities (see 2 Kg 17:24–34). It was also special because it did not require sacrifices, which were the traditional way of worshipping gods in the Mediterranean world.

Modern folks might not see the exiles' religion as unusual or unique, since it is akin to the religion practiced today: reading and studying scripture, offering prayers, and singing are the ways most modern people worship their deities.

Read 1 Chr 10.

A. How did Saul die?

B. What happened to his house?

C. What evidence can you find in this account that the Chronicler (CH) had access to the DH?

D. Why do you think the Chronicler presented a different version of history?

Read 2 Sam 11–12 and 1 Chr 20:1–3

  A. How has the CH changed the DH?

  B. Why do you think the CH made these changes?

Review 2 Kg 1 and the Solomon worksheet (Chapter 21). Read 1 Chr 23:1, 29:22b–25.

  A. How did the CH change the description of Solomon's rise to power?

  B. Why do you think the CH changed the DH's version of the story?

Review 2 Kg 6 and 7 and the Solomon worksheet (Chapter 21). Read 1 Chr 23, 28.

  A. Who is responsible for construction of the temple in the DH?

  B. Who is responsible for the construction of the temple in the CH?

  C. What personnel are added to the description of the temple in the CH?

Hezekiah

Review 2 Kg 18, the Judean Kings worksheet (Chapter 23) and read 2 Chr 29–31.

  A. List at least three changes the CH made to the DH's account of Hezekiah's reign:

    1.

    2.

    3.

  B. Who seems to be in charge of taking care of the temple?

Manasseh

Review 2 Kg 21:1–18, the Judean Kings worksheet (Chapter 23), and read 2 Chr 33.

A. List at least three major changes the CH introduced to the DH version of Manasseh's reign.

1.

2.

3.

Josiah

Review 2 Kg 22–23, the Judean Kings worksheet, and read 2 Chr 34–35.

*A. How does the CH rearrange the events of Josiah's reign?

B. Who is in charge of the repair of the Temple in the CH?

Analysis

*A. Which group or groups benefit from rewriting the DH?

*B. Why are they not mentioned in the DH, if they are so important in the CH?

*C. Why is responsibility for design of and personnel arrangement in the temple shifted?

*D. Why are changes made to the way David and Solomon ascend to the throne?

*E. Based on this analysis, what is the overarching goal of the CH?

....

FOR FURTHER READING

Ralph W. Klein, "Chronicles, Book of 1–2," *Anchor Bible Dictionary* (*ABD*) 1:992–1002.
Merlin D. Rehm, "Levites and Priests," *ABD* 4:197–210.

CHAPTER 26

Ezra/Nehemiah

Read Ezra 3–4, 6–7, 9–10:17; Neh 1–3, 6:15–19, 13

In this chapter, we will:

- Study the end of the exile and the restoration of the Jerusalem cult
- Examine how the exilic community definition of proper religious practice differed from that of the non-exiles

As with Chronicles, Ezra, and Nehemiah were written after the end of the exile, some time after 538. Most scholars date them to around 450–400 BCE. The three books may have been written by the same group, since Ezra begins where Chronicles ends.

There are numerous historical questions surrounding the figures of Ezra and Nehemiah: which man was earlier? did they know each other? when were they active?

We will not focus on these questions. Rather, we will think about what the books say about the return from the Babylonian exile, the restoration of the temple, and the sort of religion and society Ezra and Nehemiah proposed (review "Exilic Innovations" on p. 122).

End of Exile/Rebuilding Temple

Ezra 3–4, 6

A. In 538, Cyrus issued his edit, which is quoted in Ezra 1:2–3. What did it say or allow?

B. What were the stages of the restoration of the Temple?

    1. Ezra 3:1–7

    2. Ezra 3:8–13

    3. Ezra 4

        a. Who opposed the rebuilding of the temple?

        b. What argument did they make that persuaded the king to issue a "cease and desist" order?

    4. Ezra 6

        a. What allowed the rebuilding of the temple to proceed?

Ezra's Mission

Ezra 7, 9, 10:1–17

A. Where was Ezra from?

B. What was his occupation?

C. What was his goal? (7:10, 25–26)

D. How were the people in Judea *not* observing God's law? Why were they so "disobedient" (at least according to Ezra)?

E. How did the people respond to Ezra's "correction" of their behavior?

Neh 8

F. What did Ezra do here?

Nehemiah's Mission

Neh 1–3

A. Where was Nehemiah from?

B. What was his occupation?

C. What was his goal or mission in Jerusalem?

Neh 6:15–19

D. How would you characterize the relations between Tobiah and people in Jerusalem?

Neh 13

E. How popular or lasting were Nehemiah's reforms?

Analysis

A. What are some common themes or similarities between Ezra and Nehemiah's activities?

B. What were their attitudes towards the non-exiles? toward the returning exiles?

Figure 26–1. A descendant of Tobiah the Ammonite slave probably built the Iraq el-Amir, a large pleasure palace about half-way between Jericho and Ammon. This picture shows the palace, which was originally surrounded by a large lake. The lush greenery belies the notion that Israel and Jordan are all stony desert.

C. Which group (exiles or non-exiles) seemed to know how to worship correctly?

D. How did Ezra and Nehemiah relate to the ideology of the DH? (*Hint:* think about their attitudes toward foreigners)

FOR FURTHER READING

Ralph W. Klein, "Ezra-Nehemiah, Books of," *Anchor Bible Dictionary (ABD)* 2:731–42.
Robert P. Carroll, "Israel, History of: Post-Monarchic Period," *ABD* 3:567–76.

Other Literary Genres

Prophets, Poetry, Wisdom, Novellas, Apocalyptic

CHAPTER 27

Methodology

In Part Two, we studied the Deuteronomistic history at some length. In addition to being a very important set of documents in its own right, we will refer to them in two ways in Part Three:

- We will try to situate historically different pieces of literature into the time line we established in Part Two.
- We will compare the theology of the DH with that of different sorts of literature. We will see that the different biblical authors disagreed about many issues and that the DH is not the Bible's only voice.

Most of the material in Part Two could be considered "historical" narrative. We will be looking at a variety of different types of literature in Part Three. We will be classifying them into different genres, or types of literature.

Everyone is familiar with different types of literature, such as biography, science fiction, newspapers and so forth. Why is it important to try to classify biblical books into different genres?

You need to think about genre because it affects the way you interpret the data you are receiving. You do this automatically whenever you read a text or watch TV. Think of the following example:

Imagine you are watching a TV show that talks about a powerful new drug that can cure some terrible disease, but, if it were stolen by terrorists or somehow escaped from the laboratory, would cause huge numbers of deaths. Should this drug be further developed or should it be destroyed?

How do you respond to this if it is on *Nightline* or the *CBS Evening News?*

How do you respond to the story if it is on the *X-Files?*

Your response will depend on whether you think the story is fiction or news (and therefore "true"). You know that the genre of *Nightline* is very different from *X-Files* and your response to an identical story will be affected by the way you have classified the source of the story.

Genres can be large categories, such as history or prophetic materials; or small, such as different types of poems, metaphors for God's relationship to Israel, and the like. In either case, categorizing materials into different genres will assist the reader in interpreting the text.

CHAPTER 28

Prophets in the Deuteronomistic History

In this chapter, we will:

- Introduce the various types of oracles delivered by prophets
- Think about early prophets, as reported in the Deuteronomistic history

As mentioned earlier (see p. 67), Jewish tradition divides the Hebrew Bible into three parts. One of these is *Nevi'im*, or Prophets. *Nevi'im* includes the *Former Prophets*, what scholars call the Deuteronomistic history (Judges, Joshua, Samuel, and Kings) and the *Latter Prophets*. The *Latter Prophets* is comprised of the major prophets (Isaiah, Jeremiah, and Ezekiel), and the book of the 12 (Hosea through Malachi). The books in the *Latter Prophets* are arranged mainly according to their length, rather than chronologically.

We will, however, examine the prophetic writings in rough chronological sequence. The earliest prophet whose sayings were collected is Amos (active around 750 BCE). But prophets appeared much earlier in Israel's history. We begin, therefore, examining prophets in the DH, which, although composed later than Amos (review Chapter 24), reports activities of prophets as early as Samuel (active around 1000 BCE).

The subsequent three chapters will study prophets from later periods: those active during the rise of Assyria (8th century), those active during the rise of Babylon (late 7th and early 6th century), and those active during the Exile and post-exilic period (mid-6th century).

We begin by thinking about how prophets function in the DH.

Methodological Difficulties with Prophets in the DH

If one wants to learn about prophets before the eighth century prophets (Amos, Micah, Isaiah, Hosea), one can only find them in the DH. But this raises a methodological problem.

A. When was the Book of the Law found? (See chapters 23 and 24.)

B. The Kings of Israel are criticized by the DH for not worshipping as prescribed by the Book of the Law. Is this "fair"? Why or why not?

*C. Read 2 Kg 17:13–14. How does this address the issue raised in the previous question? Why are prophets so important to the DH?

D. Why do you think the prophets whose words are recorded in the DH so closely agree with the theology of the DH?

Types of Oracles

Israelite prophets delivered "oracles," which fell into three main categories. Samuel can be found doing all three. Read the following passages and try to give a descriptive name to the category.

Passage	Activity
Type 1: 1 Sam 10:1	_____
Type 2: 1 Sam 13:13	_____
Type 3: 1 Sam 15:1–3	_____

Examples of Prophetic Activity

Now look at the passages listed in Table 28–1; you may have to read a bit before and after them to understand their context. Classify them as type 1, 2, or 3. If the DH indicates the prophecy was fulfilled (and almost all type 2 or 3 is fulfilled), note the citation and roughly how long has elapsed between the prophecy and its fulfillment. Finally, note who the prophet addresses: who is his audience?

TABLE 28–1

Passage	Type	Fulfill Cite	Fulfill Time	Audience
1 Sam 15:17–23				
2 Sam 12:1–15				
2 Sam 24:1–14				
1 Kg 1:32–40				
1 Kg 11:29–39				
1 Kg 14:6–14				
1 Kg 16:1–6				
1 Kg 21:17–19				

Analysis

Look at Table 28–1 and answer the following questions:

A. Where were prophets more frequently found, in Israel or Judah?

B. Many people think that prophets predicted events in the distant future. Where does this happen on the chart?

C. Who was the audience for the prophet? Who did they interact with?

Figure 28–1. Elisha's reaction to being called "baldy" seems a bit extreme. (2 Kg 2:23–24)

Organization

Many of the prophets whose oracles are collected into books (Isaiah, Amos, and others) seem to operate alone. Was this typical?

A. Read 2 Kg 2. Who do Elijah and Elisha encounter at Bethel and Jericho?

B. Read 1 Sam 10:5, 10. How are prophets described here?

C. Read 1 Kg 18:34. Who supported the prophets?

D. Common perceptions of prophets.

    1. Read 1 Sam 19:20–21, 23–24. How are prophets described?

    2. Read 2 Kg 9:11. What did Jehu and his officers say about prophets? (Ironically, notice that the prophet's words are accepted, without debate, by the officers.)

True Prophets?

Table 28–1 demonstrated that prophets typically addressed kings. They offered the king advice or criticized him for covenant violations. But what could the king do if prophets disagreed with each other? Read 1 Kg 22:1–40.

A. Jehoshaphat and Ahab consult prophets. What do they want to know? Which oracular function are the prophets fulfilling?

B. If the situation of royal patronage seen in 1 Kg 18:3–4 was common, what sort of response might we expect the prophets to have given to queries from the king?

C. Prophets frequently acted out their prophecies. They were also able to act in ways that violated social mores (as seen above in 1 Sam 19:20–24). How does Zedekiah enact his prophecy?

D. How did Micaiah explain that his prophecy differed from those of "the prophets"?

E. If you were the king, how would you determine which course of action to follow?

FOR FURTHER READING

John J. Schmitt, "Prophecy: Preexilic Hebrew Prophecy," *Anchor Bible Dictionary* (*ABD*) 5:482–89.

CHAPTER 29

Assyrian Period Prophets

In this chapter, we will:

- Introduce the common prophetic themes we will study for the next several chapters
- Consider the prophets from the eighth century BCE

The four prophets we will discuss in this section flourished in the 8th century. This century saw two important developments. First, the kings of both Israel and Judah became more powerful and richer. This is apparent from the Biblical record. Jeroboam II (786–746 BCE) recaptured the northern parts of Israel from Aram/Syria (2 Kg 14:23–29). Archaeological evidence suggests that both Jerusalem and Samaria grew wealthier during the first half of the 8th century, but the surrounding countryside did not. These socioeconomic disparities were the topic of much prophetic attention.

The second important development was the rise of Assyria. Jeroboam II's conquests were enabled, in part, by Assyria's defeat of Aram/Syria. But after Jeroboam's death, the Assyrians continued moving south through Palestine (2 Kg 15:19–20, 29, 16:5–11, 18b, and 17:1–6), eventually destroying Israel (722 BCE) and making Judah a vassal state (2 Kg 16:6–7, 18:14–15). We will see that the prophets frequently commented on international politics.

PROBLEMS WITH PROPHETS

It is clear from the standardized introductions to the collections of prophetic oracles (Amos 1:1, Micah 1:1, Hosea 1:1, Isa 1:1, etc.) that some time after the prophets spoke, their words were collected and edited. When this happened is unknown; who the editors were is also unknown. We need to be alert to the possibility that other material—

Hebrew Poetry

While there are poems scattered throughout the Torah and Deuteronomistic history, the majority of the text is prose. Prophetic oracles are just the opposite: most of them are in poetic form.

Hebrew poetry is very different from Shakespeare's iambic pentameter or Homer's dactylic hexameter. These styles emphasize lines with the same number of syllables and accenting certain syllables in regular order. Hebrew poetry is also different from rhymed verse.

The most characteristic trait of Hebrew poetry is that lines are grouped in couplets or occasionally triplets. The lines are short (3–5 words) but the number of syllables is not fixed, nor do the lines rhyme. The lines (A and B) relate to each other in a variety of patterns:

- A and B say virtually the same thing. B emphatically restates A.
- A may start an idea and B will complete it.
- A and B may disagree. B is in opposition to A.
- A may make a statement and B pose a question.

In short, B "supports A, carries it further, backs it up, completes it, goes beyond it."[1] In translation, some of the "A and what's more B" nature of Hebrew poetry may be observable. Much is lost, however, including puns, word-plays and alliteration. Moreover, Hebrew poetry is very terse and compact but when translated into English, translators unpack compact words (as they must, to render it intelligible to Anglophones).

Some poems (such as Psalm 119 and Lam 1–4) are acrostics: each line begins successive letters from the Hebrew alphabet. This is a very restrictive form and many scholars see it, especially in Lamentations, as a way of both expressing grief but also constraining it, so as not to be overwhelmed by it. Obviously, this form is completely lost in translation.

Be alert to the variety of different forms of Hebrew poetry as we read through prophets: they were masters of this particular medium.

[1] James L. Kugel, *The Idea of Biblical Poetry: Parallelism and Its History* (New Haven: Yale University Press, 1981) 52.

perhaps from different prophets—may have been interpolated. Moreover, it is quite unlikely that the present arrangement of oracles follows the sequence in which they were delivered. Finally, as with much of the material we have examined earlier, we need to remember that the Bible preserves words from only a fraction of the prophets active in ancient Israel. Presumably, the oracles we have were preserved because they were seen as "true" and in agreement with Judean theology.

Amos

Amos is the earliest of the "classical" prophets. His exact dates are difficult to establish, but many scholars suggest a date of around 750 BCE.

Read 1:2.

Amos here alludes to the "Day of Yahweh," the day when God was expected to come forth from his dwelling place and, as the divine warrior, fight on behalf of the Israelites or Judahites. This was a popular topic for prophets, as we will see.

A. What words or concepts correspond to each other in the first half of this verse?

B. Are they exactly parallel or do we have an "A, and what's more, B" pattern?

C. How would you answer these questions for the second half of the verse?

Read 1:3–2:16.

Amos begins (1:3–2:3) with "oracles against the nations." Again, this describes the anticipated "Day of Yahweh," when God would destroy the enemies of his people. Notice, however, they are condemned *not* for attacking Israel, but for violation of covenants and the standards of warfare. Think about his rhetorical strategy.

A. What do you think the response would be from his audience for these oracles?

B. What would be the effect of following up these oracles with the one he delivers in 2:6–16?

Read 2:9–11.

A. Prophets make frequent allusion to two different sets of events in Israel's history. What does Amos allude to in this passage?

Read chapters 2 and 5.

A. What are Israel's sins?

B. What does God want of Israel?

C. Notice the distinct anti-clerical nature to Amos' oracle in 5:21–24.

D. Is the Day of Yahweh a good thing?

Read 7:10–17.

  A. Is Amos a prophet?

Micah

Micah's dates are less clear than those of Hosea, but he seems to have been active for the last quarter of the 8th century. Micah was from Moresheth, a rural community about 25 miles southwest of Jerusalem. Some scholars believe his provincial background may explain his criticism of Jerusalem (the big city).

Read Micah 1:2–7.

  A. What is being described here?

Read Chapter 3.

  A. What does Micah say about prophets?

  B. What does he say about rulers?

Read 2:1–4 and chapter 3.

  A. What are Judah's sins?

Read 6:1–8.

Micah uses another popular prophetic form here: God bringing his people to court.

  A. When God presents his case (vss. 3–5), what events are alluded to?

  B. Judah offers a defense (vss. 6–7). What is being offered?

  C. How does the response (v. 8) rebut Judah's position?

  D. What practice does this judgment condemn? Who would have lost the most from this condemnation?

Hosea

Like Amos, Hosea's dates are difficult to establish, but many scholars think Hosea was active from around 745 to 725 BCE.

Read Chapter 1.

We saw above that prophets sometimes acted out their prophecies dramatically. This chapter provides a narrative description of Hosea doing likewise.

A. Who did God command Hosea to marry?

B. Notice that all three of Hosea's (unfortunate) children are drawn into the enacting of prophecy, as he gives them symbolic names. To understand the symbolism of marrying Gomer, read chapter 2.

Read chapter 2.

In this chapter, Hosea uses a metaphor popular with the prophets, as we will see.

A. Who is the husband in these oracles?

B. Who is the adulterous wife?

C. Adultery and unfaithfulness are metaphors for Israel doing what?

Read 4:1–19.

A. What does Hosea think about priests?

Read 11:1–11.

A. What historical event does Hosea draw upon in these verses?

B. Who plays the role of Egypt in vss. 5–7? This reflects contemporary political events.

C. What does God promise in vss. 8–11?

D. What allusion does Hosea use in verse 10?

Isaiah

The book of Isaiah is thought by most scholars to be comprised of prophecies from three periods. The earliest are found in chs. 1–39 and are dated to the end of the 8th century. Second Isaiah (chs. 40–55) is a collection of oracles from the time of the Babylonian exile (586–538). Third Isaiah (chs. 56–66) is dated to the early post-exilic period (after 538 BCE). We will consider First Isaiah here, and Second and Third Isaiah in later chapters.

Isaiah is later than Amos, Micah, or Hosea and, as we will see, seems to have been aware of their messages.

Read Isaiah 1:2–20.

A. What is the form of this oracle?

B. What is God's complaint? Where have we seen a similar form and complaint?

Read Isa 3:13–15.

A. What is the form of this oracle?

B. What is God's complaint?

Read 1:21–31.

A. What is the geographic focus of this oracle?

B. What metaphor does Isaiah use for Jerusalem?

C. Is this an optimistic or pessimistic oracle?

Read 2:1–4.

   A. What is the geographic focus of this oracle?

   B. Is it optimistic or pessimistic?

Read 2:5–22.

   A. What is Isaiah's complaint against Judah?

   B. What event does he allude to, especially beginning in v. 12?

Read Isa 20:1–4.

   A. According to this narrative, how did Isaiah dramatize his prophecy?

   B. Where have we read about prophets doing something similar before?

Analysis

One way of subdividing prophets is to study the metaphors they use to describe God's relationship with Israel.

   A. What historical event do Amos and Hosea refer to?

   B. What is the main geographic focus of Isaiah's oracles?

     It is interesting that Amos and Hosea almost never mention Zion and Isaiah almost never mentions the Exodus. Thus, they drawn on different traditions or understandings of what was important about God's relationship to Israel. This is probably related to where they were from: it is hard to imagine northerners (Israelites) predicting glory for Zion/Jerusalem.

B. What are the sins of Israel or Judah—

   1. According to Amos and Micah?

   2. According to Hosea?

   3. According to Isaiah?

   4. Would the Deuteronomistic historian have agreed with these prophets in assessing where Israel and Judah were doing wrong?

C. Would any of these men want to be seen as a "prophet"? Why or why not?

FOR FURTHER READING

Bruce E. Willoughby, "Amos, Book of," *Anchor Bible Dictionary (ABD)* 1:202–212.
Delbert R. Hillers, "Micah, Book of," *ABD* 4:807–810.
C. L. Seow, "Hosea, Book of," *ABD* 3:291–97.
Christopher R. Seitz, "Isaiah, Book of: First Isaiah," *ABD* 3:472–88.

CHAPTER 30

Babylonian Period Prophets

In this chapter we will:

- Study 6th century prophets by exploring the themes introduced in the prior chapter

After the crises related to the growth of the Assyrian empire, which resulted in the destruction of Israel and the reduction of Judah to a vassal state, prophetic activity diminished (or at least the collection of prophetic sayings decreased). However, the rapid fall of the Assyrian empire, which began around 640 BCE with increasingly successful attempts by subject provinces to rebel and ended with the fall of Nineveh, its capital, in 612, marked another international crisis. In Judah, there was another burst of prophetic activity, again related to the difficult question of figuring out which way the winds of international politics were blowing.

Jeremiah

Jeremiah came from Benjamin, the smallest and southernmost of the Israelite tribes. He was a descendant of Abiathar, one of the priests who served the Jerusalem Temple when David was king. Solomon exiled Abiathar (or his son) for supporting Adonijah (1 Kg 2:26–27). Zadok, who remained the sole priest in Solomon's temple, and his descendants were strong supporters of the Davidic dynasty. Abiathar and his descendants doubtless disagreed. Jeremiah's critique of the Jerusalem cult derives, in part, from this heritage.

Jeremiah was active for a very long time. His first prophecies date to around 627 BCE and he remained active through the destruction of Jerusalem in 586 BCE.

Read Jeremiah 2:4–37.

This long poem draws on many themes we identified in the previous chapter.

147

A. What historical event does Jeremiah refer to in vss. 4–7?

B. What rhetorical device does Jeremiah employ starting in vs. 9 (see also vs. 12)?

C. What metaphor does Jeremiah use to describe God's relationship to Israel starting in vs. 20?

D. What does Jeremiah think about Judah's leaders?

Zion theology

In the previous chapter we saw that Isaiah drew upon traditions exalting Zion. The Jerusalemites seem to have thought that God would not allow his holy city to be captured, an idea that would have gained credibility after the failure of Sennacherib's siege against Jerusalem (2 Kg 19, Isa 37). Jeremiah's attitude toward this theology is evident in a late (exilic?) prose description of his preaching. Read Chapter 7:1–15.

A. What is "deceptive" about the words "This is the temple of Yahweh"? (vs. 4)

B. What are Judah's sins?

C. What is the problem with the temple worship, according to vss. 8–10?

D. Shiloh was sanctuary of Yahweh during the Judges period (Josh 18, 1 Sam 1) but it was destroyed. Why does Jeremiah mention it in his speech?

E. What may have been a different speech (vss. 21–26) has been attached to the description of the temple sermon.

1. What is the argument that is made here?

2. Where have we seen similar comments before?

Read Jeremiah 27–28.

This story is interesting for a number of reasons.

A. How common were prophets in the region around Judah? Were prophets found only in Judah?

B. Jeremiah provides advice on international politics. What does he council Judah and the surrounding kingdoms?

C. How does Jeremiah dramatically act out his prophecy?

D. When faced with two prophets, giving different messages, how did someone know who to follow?

Ezekiel

Ezekiel served a priest in the temple in Jerusalem. He was taken into exile during the first deportation (597 BCE, Ezk 1:2). While in exile, he became a prophet and offered some of the most dramatic descriptions of God found in the Hebrew Bible.

The period of his prophetic activity extended from 597 until after the fall of Jerusalem in 586 BCE.

Theophanies

A theophany is a description of the appearance of God to a visionary. We studied Elijah's theophany earlier (see p. 138). Now we consider those of Isaiah and Jeremiah.

Isaiah envisioned God sitting on a throne in the temple. He was surrounded by seraphs (a type of angelic being) with six wings, who praised him. Isaiah complained that his lips were unclean and a seraph touched his mouth with a coal from the altar. Once purified, he began to proclaim the word of God (Isa 6).

Jeremiah offered no description of the divine court or God, but says that God told him that he was predestined to be a prophet, from before his birth. Yahweh reassured Jeremiah that he would tell him what to say and touched Jeremiah's mouth, putting his words in Jeremiah's mouth (Jer 1:4–10).

There are some interesting parallels between these two accounts:

- Both Jeremiah and Isaiah are anxious about becoming prophets, but are reassured by God.
- They both see, graphically, the word of God coming to them, with something being done to their mouths.

You might review Exod 4:1–17, where Moses exhibits exactly the same traits.

Be alert for similar parallels when reading Ezekiel's far more elaborately described theophany.

Ezekiel's theophany. Read Ezek 1:1–3:11.

   A. What is Ezekiel describing in 1:5–12?

   B. What is described in 1:15–22?

   C. What is the relationship between the creatures and the wheeled vehicle?

   D. What is described in 1:26–28?

   E. Notice the language Ezekiel used here: "the *appearance* of the *likeness* of the *glory* of Yahweh." How is this different from Moses' relationship to God as described in Num 12:8?

   F. What similarities can you see between Ezekiel's commission (2:1–3:10) and those of Isaiah and Jeremiah (see p. 149)?

Read Ezek 4:1–5:4.

   A. How did Ezekiel dramatically enact his prophecies?

Read Ezek 8–9.

   A. What are the sins of the Judahites?

   B. What will God do to them?

Read Ezek 23.

   A. What historical events are alluded to here?

   B. What metaphor does Ezekiel employ to refer to God's relationship with Israel?

C. The language Ezekiel employs in this chapter has been toned down by translators, but it is still shockingly graphic. Why do you think Ezekiel used such language?

The oracles we have been considering thus far in Ezekiel were delivered before the destruction of the temple in 586 BCE. Ezek 33:21–22 reports that the news of the destruction of the temple reached the exilic community. Ezekiel's oracles shift in tone afterwards.

Read Ezek 34:1–31.

A. What is the topic of vss. 1–10? Who does it condemn?

B. What is the topic of vss. 11–16. What does it promise?

C. What is the topic of vss. 23–24? Is "shepherd" defined differently here than in vss. 1–10?

Read Ezek 37:1–6.

A. What does this prophecy promise?

B. How do Ezekiel's post-destruction oracles differ from those made before the destruction of Jerusalem?

Analysis

A. What themes or metaphors connect Jeremiah and Ezekiel to their predecessors?

B. Would Jeremiah and Ezekiel have agreed about Zion theology?

FOR FURTHER READING

Jack R. Lundbom, "Jeremiah, Book of," *Anchor Bible Dictionary* (*ABD*) 3:706–21.
Lawrence Boadt, "Ezekiel, Book of," *ABD* 2:711–22.
Jon D. Levenson, "Zion Traditions," *ABD* 6:1098–1102.

CHAPTER 31

Exilic and Post-Exilic Prophets

In this chapter, we will:

- Study the difference between exilic and post-exilic prophets and earlier prophets
- Continue to explore the themes introduced in the prior chapters

We saw previously (see Chapter 28) that several important functions of prophets were directly related to their interactions with the monarchy. After the exile, the monarchy was not restored. Judah, called Yehud in the Persian administrative system, was a small province, comprised of Jerusalem and its surrounding countryside. It was much smaller than the pre-exilic Judah. It was initially governed by governors appointed by the Persian king, such as Sheshbazzar (Ez 1:8) or Nehemiah. After some time, administration was taken over by the priests who ran the temple. The High Priest thus became the *de facto* ruler of the Judean state. This continued until the Maccabean revolt in 167 BCE.

Second Isaiah

We noted earlier (Chapter 29) that the book of Isaiah contains prophecies from three different periods. The oldest part, called First Isaiah, comes from the 8th century. Second Isaiah, chapters 40–55, collects oracles uttered in exile, probably around 550 BCE. It is these oracles we now turn to.

Political turmoil was correlated with prophecy in the Assyrian and Babylonian periods. The exilic situation was similar. Cyrus united the Persian tribes by 550 BCE and by 547 had successfully campaigned in Armenia and Asia Minor, creating the Persian Empire. It would have been apparent throughout Mesopotamia that the days of the Babylonian Empire were numbered. As usual when an empire died, there would be turmoil, especially in the Babylonian heartland, where the Judean exiles were settled. The response, again, was a burst of prophetic activity.

Read Isa 40.

  A. What does this hymn promise the exiles? Is it optimistic or pessimistic?

  B. What theme from First Isaiah is echoed in vss. 2, 9?

  C. What event is recalled in vss. 12–26?

Read Isa 45.

Earlier, it was argued that the exilic community developed new religious ideas (see box on p. 122). One important concept is evident in this chapter (and other places in Second Isaiah).

  A. How are the descriptions of Yahweh in vss. 5–8 different from the descriptions in the 10 Commandments or the Shema (see Chapter 11)?

  B. Messiahs are not unusual in the Hebrew Bible, since *messiah* means anointed. Thus, Saul, David, and other kings were all messiahs. Second Isaiah applies this language to a foreign leader. Who was it?

  C. How does this messiah relate to God?

  D. What event is recalled in vss. 18–19?

Third Isaiah

Most critical scholars think the last portion of Isaiah, chapters 56–66, was composed in Judah after the exile had ended. This prophet (perhaps the same as Second Isaiah) drew on old traditions, but also reformulated them in innovative ways.

Read Deut 23:1–8.

  A. Who is prohibited from joining the "assembly of Yahweh" in vs. 1?

  B. Who is prohibited in vss. 3–8?

Read Isa 56:1–8.

Notice the puns and double entendres, especially in vss. 3–5.

   A. How does Third Isaiah redefine the community? What is the criteria for membership?

   B. This passage echoes the theme we saw in Isa 2. What is this called?

Read Chapter 60.

   A. What does this song promise the Judeans?

   B. How will foreigners relate to Jeruslaem?

   C. What is this ideology called?

Haggai

Haggai and Zechariah were contemporaries. They were both involved in the restored community of exiles, described in Ezra 1–3. Haggai was active for six months in 520 BCE.

Read Chapter 1.

   A. What problem did Haggai address?

   B. What motivation did Haggai provide for the Jerusalemites?

   C. What was his attitude was toward priests and governors?

Zechariah

Most scholars think that Zech 1–8 and 9–14 were composed by two different individuals (or schools). Chapters 1–8 are dated from 520–518 BCE, making Zechariah a contemporary of Haggai. There is no agreement about the dates for Chapters 9–14.

Read 1:1–6.

   A. What is God's argument in 1:3–6?

B. Where have we encountered similar language?

Read 1:7–17.

  A. How is this vision of God different from those of earlier prophets? (*Hint:* how is Zechariah able to understand it?)

  B. What is the message of the vision?

Read 3:1–10.

Note that the NRSV translates *haSatan* (the satan) as a proper noun (Satan). This is incorrect, since it has a definite article and it is properly translated as a title *the accuser* or *the adversary.* We will encounter the accuser again when we get to Job.

  A. What is Joshua supposed to do?

  B. Where have we heard this sort of language before?

  C. What will God do in return?

  D. Who is the "branch" in verse 8? (*Hint:* Read Isa 11:1–3.)

  *E. What themes connect Haggai and Zechariah to the Deuteronomistic school?

Final Comments

After studying the prophets, it is interesting to note that they fall into different groups. Some prophets emphasize the Exodus traditions and failure to obey God's commandments, especially about social justice. These prophets mainly prophasied in Israel or, like Jeremiah, were not admirers of the temple in Jerusalem. Another group emphasized traditions about Zion, God's mountain in Jerusalem, and mention creation. They are more favorably inclined towards the temple.

All the prophets use similar metaphors (such as the legal suit and whoredom) to describe God's relationship with Israel. All the pre-exilic prophets condemn their leaders and priests. That the post-exilic prophets do not perhaps indicates they were court or temple prophets who worked with the leaders.

FOR FURTHER READING

John Barton, "Prophecy: Postexilic Hebrew Prophecy," *Anchor Bible Dictionary* (*ABD*) 5:489–95.

Richard J. Clifford, "Isaiah, Book of: Second Isaiah," *ABD* 3:490–501.

Christopher R. Seitz, "Isaiah, Book of: Third Isaiah," *ABD* 3:501–507.

Carol Meyers and Eric M. Meyers, "Haggai, Book of," *ABD* 3:20–23.

Carol Meyers and Eric M. Meyers, "Zechariah, Book of: Zechariah 1–8," *ABD* 6:1061–65.

David L. Petersen, "Zechariah, Book of: Zechariah 9–14," *ABD* 6:1065–1068.

CHAPTER 32

Psalms and Poetry

In this chapter, we will:

- Define a new method of interpreting the Bible: form criticism
- Apply form criticism to the Psalms
- Study different types of Hebrew poetry

We have discussed source criticism and redaction criticism in earlier chapters. Scholars have found another methodology especially rewarding for the study of Psalms: form criticism. It is widely accepted that the book of Psalms formed the "hymnal" for the temple in Jerusalem.

In all religious traditions, liturgies (religious services) are related to the calendar. Certain songs are sung for certain holidays and not sung at other times. Assuming this to be true of the Psalms, scholars would like to figure out what occasions might have been associated with the singing of particular psalms.

Unfortunately, whoever arranged the Psalms did not, apparently, group them according to their usage. In fact, a pattern to their arrangement is difficult to discern. So Biblical scholars classify psalms into different types (the exact number varies from scholar to scholar). They then look at all the psalms of one type and think about how they could have been used in the liturgical calendar of ancient Jerusalem.

We will see how this works by classifying psalms into six categories, whose names and definitions are as follows. (Note that this classification system is artificial—we could use four categories or ten, depending on how specific we would like to be about the different types of psalms.)

- Complaint—The singer tells God of some situation that requires God's help.
- Praise—The singer praises God.
- Royal—The king is the subject of the psalm.
- Thanksgiving—The singer thanks God for delivery from trouble.
- Wisdom—The singer reflects on how to live life.
- Zion—Mt. Zion (Jerusalem) is subject of the psalm.

Classification—Form Criticism

Read the following psalms and assign them to one of the six categories above.

Type	Psalms	Category
1	8, 29	_____
2	79, 83	_____
3	18, 30	_____
4	72, 89	_____
5	48, 76	_____
6	37, 49	_____

Now classify the following six psalms. Also, from your small sample set (of three psalms per category) provide additional characteristics for each class of psalm.

116	_____
123	_____
96	_____
112	_____
132	_____
87	_____

*When do you think each type of psalm might have been sung/performed/used?

Authorship and Organization

A. What type of psalms are Ps 1 and 2?

B. Who is the author of these psalms? (Note that the author is usually named before the psalm begins—see Pss 3, 4, 5, etc.)

C. Why do you think these two psalms were placed at the beginning of the collection?

Look at the following verses: 41:13, 72:18–19, 89:52, 106:48, 150:1–6.

D. How are they similar?

E. How do they function in the book of Psalms?

F. Why do you think there are five of them?

Song of Solomon / Song of Songs

We will examine the Song of Solomon to see some of the characteristics of Hebrew poetry (re-read box in Chapter 30). We will look at a few verses very closely to see how the different parts (A and B or A, B, and C) relate to one another. Sometimes these are fairly obvious; at other times (especially in translation) they are difficult to interpret. A complicating issue is the division into chapters and verses, which were not present in the original text.

If we will look at the first eight verses of chapter 1, we can observe several patterns. Read the verses and indicate how they relate to each other.

A. 1:2a: This has an A, A′ pattern. What links the two parts of the verse?

B. 1:2b-3c: These two verses have an A, B, B′, A′ pattern.

   1. What links A and A′?

   2. What links B and B′?

C. 1:4. This verse has five components, which fall into an A, A′, B, B′, C pattern.

   1. What links A and A′?

   2. What links B and B′?

   3. What is the subject of C?

D. 1:5. This verse has parts, which fall into an A, B, A′, B′ pattern.

1. What links A and A′? (*Note:* Kedar means "dark.")

2. What links B and B′?

E. 1:6. This verse has five components, which fall into an A, A′, B, C, C′ pattern.

1. What connects A and A′?

2. Does B connect to A or C?

3. What connects C and C′? Are they parallel or antithetical (opposing one another)?

F. Notice the wide variety of patterns you have seen here:

A, A′ – Parallel

A, B, B′, A′ – Chiastic

A, A′, B, B′, C – Parallel couplets

A, A′, B, C, C′ – Parallel couplets

FOR FURTHER READING

John Barton, "Form Criticism: Old Testament," *Anchor Bible Dictionary* (*ABD*) 2:838–841.
James Limburg, "Psalms, Book of," *ABD* 5:522–36.
Adele Berlin, "Parallelism," *ABD* 5:155–62.

CHAPTER 33

Wisdom

In this chapter, we will

- Discuss the issue of *theodicy* and retribution theology
- Examine wisdom literature and wisdom's responses to theodicy

Bad things happen to good people all the time. This is a special problem for people in monotheistic religious systems, since disasters cannot be attributed to malevolent deities. Why does a just God appear indifferent to the sufferings of virtuous people? The technical term for this issue is *theodicy.*

One possible answer is that of *retribution theology:* God rewards those who live according to God's law and punishes those who spurn God's commandments. But this seems refuted by observation of day-to-day life, where there is no obvious correlation between misbehavior and being destroyed by a hurricane, earthquake, or drive-by shooting.

In this chapter, we will consider the range and variety of answers offered by the biblical authors to the question of theodicy. The most complex discussions of theodicy in the Hebrew Bible are found in wisdom literature: Proverbs, Job, and Ecclesiastes/Qohelet.

Theodicy in the Deuteronomistic History

Review Deut 28 and 2 Kg 17. How did Deuteronomistic historian explain why bad things happened to Israel?

Proverbs

Read Prov 1 and 3.

Prologue (Prov. 1:1–7)

  A. Who are the proverbs attributed to?

  B. What does the prologue advise people to do?

  C. How does the prologue conclude?

Instruction

The first nine chapters of proverbs take the form of a father teaching his son (or a master his disciple). Read 1:20–33.

  A. How is wisdom personified?

  B. How hard is it to acquire wisdom?

Read 1:8–19.

  A. What sorts of activities do sinners do?

  B. What is their fate?

Read Chapter 3.

  A. What activities are associated with wisdom?

  B. What is better than gold and silver?

Saying collections. Read 10:1–7, 16:1–10.

Proverbs 10:1–22:16 are collections of sayings or aphorisms. They are short and memorable, with each verse having two parts, A and B. The collection is usually divided into two parts, 10:1–15:33 and 16:1–22:16. How are these parts different?

A. In 10:1–7, how do the two parts of the verse relate to each other? Do they agree and complement each other or disagree and oppose each other?

B. In 16:1–10, how do the two parts of the verse relate to each other?

 * According to proverbs, why do bad things happen to people? Do they seem aware of the issue of theodicy?

Job

Read Ch 1–4, 8, 11, 38–42.
The compositional history of this book is unclear. It has two different forms of writing, prose and poetry, which differ enormously in their outlook and theology. We will consider these sections separately and then reflect on their juxtaposition.

The Prose Framework (1:1–2:13, 42:7–17)

A. According to Job 1, what sort of person was Job? What sort of life should he have had, based on retribution theology?

B. What was the satan's position vis-à-vis God? (As in Zechariah, the Hebrew says *haSatan* or "the satan"—a title, not a proper name.)

C. Who called attention to Job?

D. Who was responsible for Job's suffering?

E. You may have observed the strongly parallel structure of these two chapters:

 a. 1:6–12 and 2:1–6—Discussion in heavenly court

 b. 1:13–19 and 2:7–8—Job afflicted

 c. 1:20–21 and 2:9–10a—Job's reaction

 d. 1:22 and 2:10b—Narrator's evaluation of Job

Look at the narrator's evaluations—how are they different? Is the narrator suggesting something about Job in a subtle manner?

*F. What does Ch 1–2 say about theodicy? What does it say about retribution theology?

Now read 42:7–17. It is hard to imagine this section of narrative standing without something between it and the opening prose narrative: what have Job's three friends done to offend God? (And what about the fourth friend, Elihu?) Ironically, as we will see, reading the poetic section, which *is* found between chapters 2 and 42, will not answer this question!

G. What happens to Job after he prays and sacrifices for his friends?

H. What does this suggest about retribution theology?

*I. Does the conclusion seem to agree with the opening with regard to retribution theology?

The Poetic Argument

After the narrative opening, the author of Job offers a lengthy poetic examination of theodicy. Job is approached by three friends (Eliphaz, Bildad, and Zophar) who comfort him. Each friend speaks and Job responds. This happens three times before a fourth friend (Elihu) appears and offers another opinion. Finally, God answers Job's repeated appeals that God should explain his suffering (13:22–23, 23:2–7, 30:20), by speaking out of the whirlwind. We will briefly look at the arguments offered by Job's three friends before considering God's response.

A. Summarize the arguments of Job's three friends. How do they explain Job's suffering? Would they agree with the DH or Proverbs? Or do they offer other explanations?

  a. Eliphaz (ch 4–5)

  b. Bildad (ch 8)

  c. Zophar (ch 11)

B. Throughout his dialog with his friends, Job maintains his innocence and asserts that he suffers unjustly. After repeatedly asking that God explain why he is suffering, God answers. Or does he? Read chapters 38-42:6.

    a. What is God's argument in these chapters?

    b. Does God explain Job's suffering? What is God's character like here?

    c. How does God explain theodicy?

Analysis

*A. How do the poetic sections of Job differ from the prose sections in explaining theodicy?

*B. Which sections of Job are closer to the explanations of theodicy offered by the DH or Proverbs?

Ecclesiastes/Qohelet

The book of Ecclesiastes is also known as Qohelet, from the Hebrew word in 1:1, translated as "teacher." This title is preferred by some because it differentiates the book from Ecclesiasticus (in the Apocrypha).

Verse 1:1 is also significant because it is evidence that the book has been edited after its original composition, as is also suggested by 12:9–14, as we shall see.

There is no clear pattern to the arguments made in Qohelet, although scholars have struggled to find them. For our purposes, we will read the first couple of chapters where the author examines what Proverbs regarded as marks of success. Does Qohelet agree with Proverbs?

Basic World View (1:1–11)

"Vanity" here derives from the archaic meaning of vain—worthless or futile ("That was done in vain.") and not more familiar meanings such as conceited ("You're so vain."). Most English translations also preserve a biblical idiom for superlatives: the song of songs is the best song, the king of kings is the highest king. So "vanity of vanities" means something like "completely (or utterly) worthless."

A. What is Qohelet's basic view of the world?

B. What is the end of all things?

Consideration of Indicators of Success (1:12–2:11)

We saw above that Proverbs extolled wisdom and hard work; in the prose introduction to Job, Job was rich, just, and upright.

A. What does Qohelet say about wisdom?

B. What does Qohelet say about material possessions?

After these assertions, doesn't Qohelet contradict himself? Read 2:12–26.

C. What does Qohelet say about wisdom and wealth?

D. What's the problem with wealth and wisdom?

E. How would Qohelet explain theodicy? Would he agree with Proverbs?

Editing?

Many scholars think Qohelet was edited especially at the introduction and conclusion. But if it was edited, perhaps other phrases were added, too. Many scholars point to 2:26 or 3:17a as examples of such interpolations. Why would they suspect that these verses were written by someone other than Qohelet? Read 11:7–12:14.

A. Where do the words of Qohelet end?

B. How is this indicated?

C. What does the epilogue (the material added to the book after the words of Qohelet) say about theodicy? About wealth and wisdom?

D. Does it agree with the words of Qohelet?

FOR FURTHER READING

Roland E. Murphy, "Wisdom in the Old Testament," *Anchor Bible Dictionary* (*ABD*) 6:920–931.

James L. Crenshaw, "Proverbs, Book of," *ABD* 5: 513–20.

James L. Crenshaw, "Job, Book of," *ABD* 3:858–868.

James L. Crenshaw, "Ecclesiastes, Book of," *ABD* 2:271–280.

James L. Crenshaw, "Theodicy," *ABD* 6:444–47.

CHAPTER 34

Esther, Jonah, and Ruth

Read Esther, Jonah, and Ruth.

In this chapter, we will:
- Define "novella" and study three examples of this type of literature
- Think about the theologies of the three authors of these novellas

In addition to history and overtly religious materials (like the words of the prophets or the hymns in the Psalter), the Bible has several short stories, sometimes called novellas. In this chapter and the next we will look at five stories: Esther, Jonah, Ruth, Tobit, and Judith.

We will try to answer several questions about these stories:

1. What was the goal of the story? (Entertainment, education, religious instruction, etc.)

2. What sort of literature is it? (History, drama, satire, humor, folk tale, fairy tale, etc.)

3. How does the outlook of the story compare to that of other biblical narratives, especially the Deuteronomistic history?

Our basic methodology will be to read these short books in their entirety, and to study the first couple of chapters of these books very closely, since most ancient authors introduced their major themes early in their works.

Esther

Chapter 1

Verses 1–9 emphasize the wealth and splendor of the Persian court.

A. The Persian Empire was comprised of 20 satrapies, or provinces. How many does Esther 1:1 say it contained?

B. How long did the feast Ahasuerus held for his officials last?

C. What is the scenario outlined by Memucan?

D. What did the decree of the king command?

*E. How probable are these events? How would the decree have been enforced?

*F. What sort of story is the author suggesting we are going to read?

Improbable elements such as those in Chapter 1 permeate the story.

A. Is Hamen's response to Mordecai's offense appropriate (Ch 3:1–6)?

B. If a cubit is 18 inches or ½ meter, how tall is the gallows Hamen erects? Approximately how tall are gallows usually?

C. Is the description of the king's edicts (8:8) a recipe for good governance?

D. Does the king's counter-order (8:11) seem like one a government would actually issue?

Literary Elements

Esther has many literary twists to the story.

A. Who constructs the gallows and for whom? Who gets hung on the gallows?

Figure 34–1. Dore's illustration of the denouement of the book of Esther, when Esther accuses Hamen before the king of plotting to kill the Jews.

B. Who describes how the king's favorite should be honored? Who gets honored?

C. What is Hamen's goal in 8:7? What does the king see? What is the outcome?

Religiosity?

Jews set themselves apart from their gentile neighbors in the ancient world by their observance of Torah, including resting on Shabbat, avoiding ritually impure foods, and refusing to worship Gods other than Yahweh. This encouraged them to marry other Jews, which was also encouraged by Deuteronomy and leaders such as Ezra and Nehemiah.

A. In light of this, what is surprising about 2:9?

B. What would the DH have thought about Esther marrying Ahasuerus?

C. How pious are Esther and Mordecai?

Evaluation

A. Who would have written and read this story?

B. Is this story anything more than simple entertainment?

C. How does the outlook of this story compare to other biblical narratives?

Jonah

Chapter 1

A. We have seen that many prophets were initially reluctant to be prophets (even Moses). How is Jonah's reluctance different from that of other prophets?

B. Tarshish was a town in Spain. Why does the author have Jonah flee there rather than, say, Egypt?

C. How is the storm described in Ch 1?

D. How did it affect the ship?

E. What was Jonah's response to the storm?

F. How is the fish described?

G. What is the response of the sailors to Jonah's testimony after throwing him overboard?

The themes found in chapter 1 are repeated throughout the book.

A. How large is Nineveh? (What modern city is this large?)

B. Jonah walks a third of the way into a foreign city and utters five words. What is the response?

This book could be interpreted in many different ways. We will think about two complementary ideas.

Jonah Compared to Other Prophets

A. Jonah makes two public pronouncements (to the sailors and to the Ninevites). What is their common response?

B. Other prophets we studied spoke to Israelites. What response did they elicit?

C. How would you describe Jonah's character? Is he a nice person?

D. How does he compare to other prophets?

E. What point could the author be making about prophets?

Tribal God?

We saw above, especially in the Exodus and Conquest narratives, that Yahweh was the God of the Israelites and condoned genocide against non-Israelites.

A. Is this the way Jonah viewed Yahweh?

B. What is God's argument in 4:10–11?

C. Does the author of Jonah agree with the Deuteronomistic historian about whom God cares for?

Evaluation

A. Who would have written and read this story?

B. Is this story anything more than simple entertainment?

C. How does the outlook of this story compare to other biblical narratives?

Ruth

Chapter 1

A. The first five verses quickly establish the main characters, Naomi and Ruth. What is significant about Ruth and Orpah?

B. What is emphasized again in vss. 10, 15, 16, and 22?

C. How is the tone of Ruth 1 different from Esther 1 or Jonah 1?

Themes

A. Hamen was villainous, Jonah was petulant. Is there a villain in this story?

B. Esther never mentioned God; Jonah had dialogues with Yahweh. How is God described here?

C. Read Deut 23:3. Why is this verse relevant to this story?

D. The story has a happy ending, when Ruth gives birth to Boaz's child. What is significant about her grandson?

Evaluation

A. Who would have written and read this story?

B. Is this story anything more than simple entertainment?

C. How does the outlook of this story compare to other biblical narratives?

FOR FURTHER READING

Carey A. Moore, "Esther, Book of," *Anchor Bible Dictionary (ABD)* 2:633–43.
Jonathan Magonet, "Jonah, Book of," *ABD* 3:936–42.
Phyllis Trible, "Ruth, Book of," *ABD* 5:842–47.

CHAPTER 35

Tobit and Judith

Read Tobit and Judith.

In this chapter, we read two more Jewish novellas, Tobit and Judith, using the same techniques we used for Esther, Jonah, and Ruth.

What is the Apocrypha?

The selections for this chapter come from the Apocrypha. What is the Apocrypha, and why is it stuck between the Hebrew Bible and the New Testament?

The Hebrew Bible (what Christians call the Old Testament) was originally written in Hebrew. But starting with the Babylonian Exile, there were significant populations of Jews living far from Judah/Judea. These communities (called the diaspora) used local vernaculars rather than Hebrew and, in time, forgot how to speak Hebrew. In response, the Bible was translated into different languages.

The most significant translation (at least from a Christian perspective) was the translation into Greek. This translation, the Septuagint, includes some works which may have been originally composed in Palestine and written in Hebrew or Aramaic (such as 1 Macc), but which exist today only in Greek. It also includes other works that were originally written in the diaspora by Greek-speaking Jews. Whatever their origin, these documents came to be considered inspired by ancient Jews, at least those in the diaspora. The Septuagint was "scripture" for the earliest Christians: when they quoted scripture, they quoted the Septuagint, not the Hebrew Bible.

After the destruction of the temple in Jerusalem (70 CE), the rabbis debated what constituted the canon. They eventually decided that one of the characteristics of "scripture" was that it be written in Hebrew. They rejected those documents found only in Greek from their canon of scripture.

But the Septuagint remains the "Old Testament" for Eastern Orthodox Christianities (which use Greek). When Jerome translated the Septuagint and New Testament into Latin, to create the Vulgate (the Bible for the Western Catholic Church), he included all the books found in the Septuagint. The Catholic and Orthodox Old Testament, then, follows the arrangement of the Septuagint.

During the Reformation, Protestants revived doubts about inspired quality of books in the Bible that were not found in the Hebrew canon. They labeled these books the Apocrypha and physically separated them, grouping them together, and placing them either between the Old Testament and the New Testament or at the very end of the Bible, after the New Testament.

In short, then, the Apocrypha are books found in the Greek version of the Old Testament but not in the Hebrew Bible. Jews do not view them as scripture; Catholic and Orthodox Christians regard them as scripture; and Protestants view them as non-canonical but valuable for spiritual edification.

179

Tobit

In Chapter 1, the initial two verses describe the setting of the story—Tobit is a member of one of the "ten lost tribes" taken into exile by the Assyrians.

   A. What does the author establish in 1:4–8?

   B. What is the significance of 1:9?

   C. What is the significance of 1:11?

   D. What is the result of these practices in 1:12–13?

   E. Based on these examples, what might we expect one of the major themes of the book to be?

Tobit continues his exemplary behavior in Chapter 2, until a disaster befalls him.

   A. What is the disaster?

   B. What is his response in 3:1–6?

In 3:7–9, the female protagonist is introduced.

   A. What is notable about Sarah?

   B. Where have we encountered evil demons in the Hebrew Bible before this?

   C. What is Sarah's response to her problem?

In 3:16–17, another major actor is introduced.

   A. Raphael means "God has healed." Why is this name appropriate for him in the context of the story?

B. Where have we encountered an angel with a name in the Hebrew Bible? Remember, the Hebrew Bible uses "satan" as a title ("*the* satan" = "the accuser"), not as a name (except in 1 Chr 21:1).

C. Angels have access to divine knowledge. What does Raphael teach Tobias in chapter 6?

D. What does he teach in chapter 12?

Literary Genres

A. What sort of literature is 4:1–19?

B. Different from Esther?

   a. What do Tobias and Sarah do before consummating their marriage?

   b. What does Raguel, Sarah's father, do when he learns that Tobias survived his wedding night?

   c. What does Tobit say when his sight is restored?

C. How are these practices different from those found in Esther?

Evaluation

A. Who would have written and read this story?

B. Is this story anything more than simple entertainment?

C. How does the outlook of this story compare to other biblical narratives?

Judith

Chapter 1

   A. What was Nebuchadnezzar's nationality? (See 2 Kg 24:1.)

   B. What is the historical problem with Judith 1:1, 1:7?

   C. How large are the walls around Ecbatana? Does this seem realistic?

* The author signals the reader what sort of literature Judith is from the beginning of the book. What is being suggested here?

   D. In addition to these historical problems, look at 4:3. How were the Assyrians (or Babylonians) chronologically related to the exile and return from exile? The same problem appears in Achior's speech in Chapter 5.

The Character of Judith

The defeat and destruction of the huge walls of Ecbatana demonstrate the overwhelming might of Nebuchadnezzar. The power of the Assyrians and Holofernes is further attested by chapters 2–7, when Holofernes finally arrives outside the walls of Bethulia.

   A. What is the response of the city's inhabitants?

   B. Judith is introduced in 8:1–8. What is emphasized or important about her?

   C. What is Judith's argument to Bethulia's elders?

   D. What does Judith do before going to Holofernes' camp?

   E. What does she take with her to his camp?

Judith and Holofernes

When you read chapters 11 and 12, notice the author's skillful use of double entendres. Does Judith lie to Holofernes? Who is her "lord"?

A. What does Judith eat and drink in the Assyrian camp?

B. What does Judith do before beheading Holofernes?

World-View

A. Achior testifies to Holofernes in 5:5–21. What does he recount? What is his theology (see esp. 5:17–18)?

B. What sort of theology is reflected in Judith's argument to Bethulia's elders?

C. What sort of theology is represented in Judith's speech to Holofernes?

Evaluation

A. Who would have written and read this story?

B. Is this story anything more than simple entertainment?

C. How does the outlook of this story compare to other biblical narratives?

FOR FURTHER READING

James H. Charlesworth, "Apocrypha: Old Testament Apocrypha," *Anchor Bible Dictionary (ABD)* 1:292–94.

Carey A. Moore, "Tobit, Book of," *ABD* 6:585–94.

Carey A. Moore, "Judith, Book of," *ABD* 3:1117–25.

CHAPTER 36

Maccabees

In this chapter, we will:

- Use historical method to understand the Maccabean revolt
- Think about the different goals of the authors of 1 and 2 Maccabees

HISTORICAL INTRODUCTION

The Persian Empire, founded by Cyrus the Great in 550 BCE, controlled Palestine until Alexander the Great's conquests (see the historical sketch at the beginning of Part Two, p. 72).

Alexander, from Macedonia, just north of Greece, attacked the Persians, led by Darius III. He defeated Darius twice in Asia Minor (in 334 and 333 BCE). Darius fled east and Alexander fought him again in Iraq in 331, prompting Darius to retreat further east. Before following Darius, Alexander turned south and marched down the Mediterranean coast to Egypt.

Most of the cities along the way welcomed Alexander. Given his military dominance, this was prudent. The Judeans also welcomed him, according to the ancient Jewish historian Josephus. During the winter, Alexander went to Egypt, where he crowned himself Pharaoh and established the new city of Alexandria. Alexandria became one of the most important cities in the Hellenistic and Roman periods and came to have a very sizable Jewish population.

Alexander followed Darius eastward, defeated him in 330, and then continued to march to the Indus River, in the northwest part of the Indian subcontinent. After his army protested this prolonged campaign (326), he turned back and died in Babylon in 323.

Alexander's empire fell apart immediately as his leading generals fought for regional control. After about 25 years of civil war, four kingdoms were established on the remains of Alexander's empire. The two that are significant for Palestine are the kingdom established in Egypt by Ptolemy (called the Ptolemaic kingdom) and the one established in Syria by Seleucus (called the Seleucid kingdom).

From around 300 until around 200, Palestine was under the control of the Ptolemies in Egypt. But their control was contested by the Seleucids, who fought a series of five wars to wrest away control of the region. Finally, Antiochus III (the Great) decisively defeated the Ptolemaic forces, and the Seleucids took over Palestine.

Antiochus III died in 187 BCE and was succeeded by his son Seleucus IV, who ruled from 187–175. Antiochus IV (Epiphanes) succeeded Seleucus (his brother) and ruled from 175–163. Antiochus is the Greek-Syrian king who 1 and 2 Maccabees mention.

Alexander is commonly remembered for his policies of *Hellenization,* which tried to get local indigenous populations to adopt some Greek mores. Alexander did not live long enough to encourage this policy systematically.

The Ptolemies did not pursue this goal aggressively either. They had the luxury of ruling a kingdom with one primary language and ethnic group. Egypt had been ruled by a central government for over a thousand years. The Ptolemies replaced an Egyptian dynasty with a Greek one, but took over much of the administrative organization of the older Egyptian kingdom.

The Seleucids, on the other hand, had a kingdom that encompassed many different peoples. It included Babylonians, Assyrians, Persians, Syrians, and eventually Jews. Each group had its own language, laws, and traditions. As a way to unite these various regions and groups, the Seleucids founded many new cities, based on Greek models. There were some Greeks living in them, but the majority of their citizens were locals, probably elites of the indigenous population. They had the institutions typical of a Greek city: a body of (free, male) citizens, streets organized on a grid, gymnasium, an *agora,* and temples for the city's gods. They encouraged the use of the Greek language. But although Greek became widely used by the urban elite (especially during the Roman period), it never replaced local vernaculars for the common people.

In 167, the Judeans rebelled against the Seleucid king. What prompted their rebellion is unclear, as we will see in this chapter. They came to be lead by a family of priests, known as the Maccabees. Antiochus IV was far more concerned with his eastern border, where the Parthian empire was growing in power, and sent only a small part of his army to Judea to suppress the rebellion. After several years, the Maccabees were able to force the Seleucids to recognize their leadership and they took over the high priesthood, becoming the governors of Judea for the Seleucid empire.

In this chapter, we will read two different ancient histories about the Maccabean revolt. We will consider their explanations for why the Jews rebelled. We will also ask how their goals were similar or different.

Read 2 Macc 4–6:17.

Jason

A. How did Jason become high priest?

B. In addition to the office, he also purchased the right to establish two other things in Jerusalem. What are they?

1.

2.

C. What does the author of 2 Macc use as examples of "extreme Hellenization"?

1.

2.

3.

4.

D. Did the author like or dislike Jason and his program?

E. What evidence can you find that Jason's contemporaries found his program offensive? Who resisted it?

Menelaus

A. How did Menelaus become high priest?

B. What happened to Jason?

C. What did Menelaus do that irritated Onias?

D. How did the Jews demonstrate they found the program of Menelaus and Lysimachus offensive?

Civil War

A. What was the rumor about Antiochus in chapter 5?

B. What prompted Jason's return to Jerusalem?

C. What happened when Jason returned?

D. How did Antiochus respond to Jason's attack? Does this seem appropriate? (You might think of international politics during the Cold War: if a nation had attacked a Soviet ally in Eastern Europe, how would the Soviet Union have responded?)

Suppression of Judaism

A. What did Antiochus do to suppress Judaism?

Read 1 Macc 1–2.

A. If Jason and/or Menelaus was the villain of 2 Maccabees, who is the villain of 1 Maccabees?

B. Who were his allies in Jerusalem? What did they do?

C. Why did Antiochus attack Jerusalem?

D. Paganism is typically tolerant. You worship Zeus, I worship Apollo, she worships Ares, he worships Athena. Since there was not "one true God," pagans rarely waged *religious* wars. If this is true, what is odd about 1 Maccabees' explanation of why Antiochus tried to suppress Judaism?

E. What did he do to suppress Judaism?

F. 1 Maccabees describes two different responses to this. What were they?

   1.

   2.

G. What was the response of Mattathias? Was he fighting for religious freedom?

H. How did the pious Mattathias and his friends reinterpret Sabbath law?

I. Who is the hero of this account?

Analysis

A. Do these two accounts agree on who the villain was?

B. Do they agree about the sequence of events leading up to the prohibition of Judaism?

C. How do you think Antiochus knew *how* to prohibit Judaism? (*Hint:* if you wanted to prohibit a religion about which you knew little, how would you know how to do it?)

D. Following 2 Maccabees, can you think of a reason Antiochus would want to prohibit Judaism?

E. The reason 1 Maccabees provides for the prohibition (1 Mac 1:41–2) is not plausible, given what is known of Antiochus and non-Jewish kings in general. Why does the author provide this reason?

*F. What is the goal of 1 Maccabees?

*G. What is the goal of 2 Maccabees? (*Hint:* look at 6:12–17.)

FOR FURTHER READING

Thomas Fischer, "Maccabees, Books of: First and Second Maccabees," *Anchor Bible Dictionary* (*ABD*) 4:439–450.

Uriel Rappaport, "Maccabean Revolt," *ABD* 4:433–39.

R. D. Milns, "Alexander the Great," *ABD* 1:146–50.

John Whitehorne, "Antiochus," *ABD* 1:269–72.

CHAPTER 37

Daniel

Read Daniel 1–3, 6–8, 11:31–12:13.

In this chapter, we will:

- Consider the compositional history of Daniel
- Define and study an early example of an apocalypse

Most scholars think Daniel is the last book of the Old Testament to have been written. Most date its final composition to the period of the Maccabean revolt, although parts of it were probably written earlier. We will first think about its compositional history before looking at why scholars think it was written during the Maccabean revolt.

Read Daniel 1, 3, and 6.

A. What is the moral or point of the story in Chapter 1?

B. What is the moral of the stories in chapters 3 and 6?

C. What do you think was the goal of the writer of these stories?

D. Can you think of parallels to these stories in other places in the Bible?

Read Daniel 2.

A. What is unreasonable about Nebuchadnezzar's request?

B. What is the response of his wise men?

C. What is Daniel's response?

D. What is the point of this story?

Read Daniel 8.

Review the historical sketch at the beginning of the Maccabees chapter and the "Symbolic History" box.

A. What did the horns on the goat represent?

   1.

   2.

Symbolic History

Daniel uses symbolism to recount (or predict) history several times. The first time is in chapter 2, with Nebuchadnezzar's dream. Modern readers may be unfamiliar with ancient world history, but Daniel's original audience in the early second century BCE would have been able to understand it with little effort.

Nebuchadnezzar's dream is about a statue that symbolizes the kingdoms that will succeed him.

- Golden head: Nebuchadnezzar
- Silver chest and arms: Median
- Bronze middle and thighs: Persian
- Iron legs: Alexander the Great
- Iron and clay feet: Alexander's successors, the Seleucid and Ptolemaic kingdoms
- Kingdom of God

How do scholars know how to interpret these symbols? The Persian empire was stronger and longer lasting than the Babylonian or Median empires, so it is depicted with a stronger metal. Alexander the Great's empire, although short lived, was the biggest empire ever seen in the ancient world, stretching from India to Greece. Alexander's strength is represented by the strongest metal known in the ancient world, iron. Alexander's empire was replaced by four smaller kingdoms, led by Greeks, but not as strong. Hence, the feet, which are Greek (iron) but are weaker (clay).

We will examine two other symbolic depictions of history below.

B. What did the male goat/ram represent? Why did it fly over the earth (8:5)?

C. Why do four horns appear on the head of the ram?

D. Who is the arrogant horn?

E. What will the arrogant horn do?

Read Daniel 7.

A. What do the four beasts look like? What do they represent?

   1.

   2.

   3.

   4.

B. Who did the little horn, who spoke arrogantly and who "change[d] the sacred time and the law," represent?

C. What did Daniel predict would happen to the little horn?

D. How is God (the Ancient One) described?

Daniel describes history again in chapters 11–13. Starting in 11:31, he describes the persecutions of Antiochus.

A. What will happen to the Jews, according to 11:32–35?

B. Beginning in 11:40, Daniel predicts the future. What does he foresee for Antiochus?

C. At the height of Antiochus' power, God intervenes in history. Who will help Israel?

D. At the end of time (chapter 12: 1–4)

    1. Who will be delivered?

    2. What will happen to the dead?

    3. When will this happen? (See 12:7, 11, 13.)

E. What is Daniel told to do with his prophecies?

Apocalypse

The book of Daniel is an example of an early apocalypse. The word *apocalypse* means revelation. What is revealed is otherworldly knowledge, usually mediated by a divine figure. Since the knowledge is heavenly, it should not be widely disseminated. The knowledge usually includes a description of a tour of heaven and/or a description of history and the future. Apocalypses use symbolic language to express the divine knowledge. Apocalypses usually expect salvation at the end of the world (eschaton) and most expect the world to end very soon (imminently).

Apocalypses were Jewish literature that first appeared in the third or second century BCE, although they have connections to older Jewish traditions, such as the Day of Yahweh we saw in the prophetic literature. They were usually written at times of oppression to provide comfort for their audiences ("You are suffering now, but bear up, because God will avenge your suffering by destroying your persecutors").

Analysis

A. Many scholars think the first six chapters of Daniel circulated independently, before being attached to Daniel 7–12. What evidence can you find for this? (*Hint:* think about the genres of the stories in each section of Daniel—are they the same?)

B. Most scholars think Daniel is the latest book of the OT to be composed and believe it was written during the persecutions of Antiochus IV (167–164 BCE). Why do you think they believe this? If they are correct, why do you think the author of Daniel placed his hero in the Assyrian court?

FOR FURTHER READING

John J. Collins, "Daniel, Book of," *Anchor Bible Dictionary* (*ABD*) 2:29–37.

Pierre Briant, "Persian Empire," *ABD* 5:236–44.

Paul D. Hanson, "Apocalypses and Apocalypticism: Introductory Overview," *ABD* 1:280–282.

Paul D. Hanson, "Apocalypses and Apocalypticism: Early Jewish Apocalypticism," *ABD* 2:282–288.

PART FOUR

New Testament

The Gospels

CHAPTER 38

New Testament Background

HISTORY

After the Maccabean revolt (167–164 BCE), which is described in 1 and 2 Maccabees and Daniel, the Maccabees ruled Judea. They came to be known as the Hasmoneans. Initially, they replaced the old high priestly families and ruled Judea, with the approval (and oversight) of the Seleucid kings.

But starting in the 130s, the Seleucid empire slipped into an extended period of civil wars, as different pretenders claimed the throne. As central authority declined, ambitious local leaders claimed autonomy and established independent kingdoms. Thus, the Hasmoneans became both high priests and kings. When Judea became independent is debated, but it certainly was by 125 BCE since the Hasmoneans began to conquer their neighbors. The Hasmonean state was relatively short lived: in 63 BCE, the Roman general Pompey conquered Syria and Palestine.

Although short lived, the success of the Hasmoneans and the Maccabean revolt was remembered by Jews as demonstrating that, with God's assistance, they would be able to throw off the yoke of mighty empires. (Modern, secular historians attribute the success of the Maccabean revolt to the fact that the Seleucids were far more concerned with limiting the expansion of the Parthian empire to their east than suppressing a rebellion in a relatively minor and unimportant western province.) This ideology and expectation helped shape the Jewish response to domination by the Roman empire.

After Pompey conquered the Hasmonean state, he appointed a Hasmonean, Hyrcanus II, to be High Priest. More significantly, he also appointed Hyrcanus' political adviser, Antipas, to an administrative position. Antipas was the father of Herod the Great, who the Romans made king of Judea in 40 BCE. King Herod ruled from 40 BCE to 4 BCE. Herod was lucky in military conflicts, a gifted politician and, although hated by some of his subjects (both Jew and Gentile), he maintained the peace in a troublesome region. The birth of Jesus is dated by Matthew (Mt 2:1) to the reign of Herod the Great.

199

Figure 38–1. Herod the great is remembered as an energetic builder, but many of his palaces were situated on top of buildings erected by the Hasmoneans. Macherus, across the Dead Sea from Qumran, is one example of this. It demonstrates the flair the Hasmoneans and Herod had for situating their palaces in dramatic locals. It is probably where Herod Antipas executed John the Baptist.

Herod was succeeded by his sons Herod Antipas, who ruled Galilee and Peraea; Archaelus, who ruled, briefly, Judea; and Herod Philip, who ruled the region northeast of the Sea of Galilee. Herod Antipas is the Herod we encounter in the gospels; he was responsible for beheading John the Baptist. Adding to the confusion of having multiple Herods, Mark incorrectly calls Herod Antipas King Herod (Mk 6:14, 22), although Herod Antipas was never granted this title by Rome.

Archaelus was incompetent, and the Romans deposed him in 6 CE. Subsequently, they administered the region of Judea with prefects from 6 CE to 41 and procurators from 44 to 66. These officials were Roman citizens, with some administrative experience, but not as much as the Senators who governed larger provinces. Good prefects maintained the peace and were relatively honest administrators; bad ones accepted bribes, administered justice poorly, and provoked their subjects. The worst, according to ancient sources, was Pilate, who governed Judea from 26 to 36 CE.

Rome's misadministration eventually sparked a revolt by the Jews, which started in 66 CE. According to Josephus, some Jewish leaders opposed the revolt, because they realized its hopelessness. Remarkably, the rebels enjoyed some initial success in 66. But by the spring of 67, Rome had organized her forces and sent Vespasian to quell the uprising. By June of 68, the whole country was under Roman control, apart from Jerusalem. It is likely that the revolt would have ended relatively soon, but events in Rome interfered.

When Nero died in June of 68 CE, Vespasian put the war effort on hold, awaiting further developments. After a year, which saw several different men hold the office of Emperor, Vespasian's troops proclaimed him emperor (in July 69). Vespasian traveled Rome in the summer of 70 to become emperor and allowed his son, Titus, to continue the war.

After this hiatus, Titus began to besiege Jerusalem in the spring of 70, and by summer had captured the whole city and temple, which was destroyed.

After the destruction of Jerusalem and the temple, the Romans had to conquer a few remaining fortresses, including Machaerus and Masada, which took until 73.

JEWISH WORLD VIEW: APOCALYPTICISM

By the first century BCE, many Jews had rejected the retribution theology espoused by the Deuteronomistic historian and other authors in the Hebrew Bible. They recognized that God did not appear to mete out rewards and punishments to the living. But rather than abandon retribution theology, they projected it into the future. God will intervene in history (as predicted by the prophets) some time in the future. When that happened, God would punish the evil and reward the good. This dramatic and considerable shift in cosmology could have been a response to the persecutions of Antiochus Epiphanes, which sparked the Maccabean revolt. He punished Jews not for disobeying God, violating commandments, or other actions deserving of punishment according to Deuteronomy, but for observing Jewish customs and Law. How could this be? Some Jews, perhaps most, came to see the current world as dominated by Satan.

The satan, who had been an obedient member of God's court in the Hebrew Bible (Job 1–2), changed. Rather than a title, Satan became a proper name, the opponent of God and the leader of the current age. Jews went back through the Bible and reinterpreted it in light of this new understanding and Satan became associated with earlier opponents of God. God was still ultimately in control, but for some unknown reason allowed Satan to dominate the current age.

This evil state would not last. Soon, very soon, God would assert himself and destroy Satan and Satan's minions, the worldly powers, to establish his kingdom and to establish his people as rulers. Scholars call this world-view *apocalypticism*, a term which means *revealed* or *unveiled*. Apocalyptic Jews (and Christians) believed that God had revealed the future to them.

Apocalyptic literature reflects this world view. Different groups of Jews had different interpretations of the future. Some thought that God would achieve his re-creation of the world by sending a human *messiah*—a warrior king (like David) who would lead Israel into battle against the forces of evil and triumph over them. Others expected a cosmic *messiah*, sometimes called the "Son of Man," a deliverer who would engage in supernatural warfare against the enemies of the Jews (as in Dan 7:9–14). This new world was frequently referred to as the "Kingdom of God."

JEWISH GOVERNANCE

One result of the Maccabean revolt was the development of Jewish sectarianism. At the time of Jesus, there were several distinct groups of Jews.

Sadducees

The Sadducees were mostly of priestly ancestry. They were of the upper class and were closely associated with the temple in Jerusalem. They were recognized by the Romans as the leaders of the Jews and advised the high priest on policy. They did not believe in resurrection of the dead (Mk 12:18).

Pharisees

The Pharisees were experts in legal interpretation of the Torah. They advocated strict observation of purity regulations as set forth in Torah as they interpreted it. The Pharisees believed in a future resurrection as well as angels and spirits (Acts 23:7–9).

Essenes

The Essenes were a small group of Jews who split away from the Jerusalem temple because they disapproved of the non-Zadokite priests who served in it during the Hasmonean period. Their ideas are known from the Qumran scrolls (or Dead Sea Scrolls), but the Essenes are not prominent in the New Testament.

In addition to these groups known from ancient sources outside the New Testament, there are several groups mentioned in the different gospels.

Scribes

Scribes were literate. They studied and taught Torah. They are frequently associated with the Pharisees.

Herodians

Little is known of this group, since they are mentioned only by Mark. Presumably Mark is referring to people allied with Herod's descendants, who ruled parts of Palestine from 40 BCE to around 90 CE (see above, History).

Chief Priests

The chief priests were the pinnacle of Jerusalem society. They ran the temple and were probably connected with the Sadducees. The high priest was the official representative of the Jews to the Roman government.

The vast majority of Jews were not associated with any of these different groups and their beliefs and practices are difficult to ascertain.

CHAPTER 39

Introduction to the Gospels

We will start exploring the New Testament by examining the Gospels. This is not the only approach we could use, since to be strictly chronological, we would start with the letters of Paul, which are the oldest documents in the New Testament. But as we will see when we examine Paul's writings, Paul says almost nothing about Jesus' life and teachings. Hence, we will begin with documents that *do* describe Jesus.

All the Gospels are anonymous. Unlike the letters of Paul, in which Paul identifies himself as the author, nowhere in the Gospels do their authors identify themselves by name. The leaders of the church in the following century assigned the names to the Gospels that we use today. And, although many scholars doubt these attributions, they continue to use the traditional names for clarity and convenience. We will follow this convention as well.

In addition to being uncertain about who wrote the gospels, scholars are not sure when they were written. The most widely accepted model suggests that Mark was written around 70 CE, since Mark 13 seems to refer to the destruction of the Temple by the Romans. Matthew and Luke were written perhaps 10–15 years later (80–85 CE), and John sometime after that (85–90 CE). Note that this means that the earliest written source we have about Jesus' life dates to some 40 years after his death. This makes it unlikely that any of the gospels were composed by Jesus' disciples or other eyewitnesses to his ministry. We will consider the implications of this important fact when we discuss the historical Jesus.

By the time the Gospels were written, there was growing tension between traditional Jews and those who believed Jesus to be messiah, who came to be called Christians. Jesus preached to Jews and all his disciples were Jews. After his death, his followers continued to preach to Jews, but eventually expanded their mission to include Gentiles as well. Why did they do this?

It may have been inspired by the Jewish idea that in the Kingdom of God, all nations would worship the God of Israel (Isa 2:2–4, 56:1–8, etc). Or perhaps, finding a skeptical reception among Jews, they sought a wider audience.

In any case, by the time the gospels were written, although some of the followers of Jesus were Jews, many (perhaps a majority?) were gentiles, especially outside of

Palestine. This situation was a puzzle for the gospel writers. They struggled to understand and explain why Jesus, a Jew, who preached to Jews in Galilee and Judea, who attracted a band of Jewish disciples, who directed his disciples to go only to the lost sheep of the house of Israel (Matt 10:6), and who preached a message about the Jewish God intervening in human history as predicted by Jewish scriptures, found a more receptive audience among non-Jews. The different gospel writers offered different answers to this very puzzling question, as we will see.

When did the two groups split apart decisively? No one knows, in part because, as pointed out above, until 70 CE there were many different sects of Judaism, and Christians were one of them. Later, there were many different sects of Christians, some of whom advocated a complete break with Jews and Jewish scripture (like Marcion, see Chapter 52), and others who continued to observe Jewish customs such as circumcision and kosher food laws, while hailing Jesus as the savior and messiah (like the author of Matthew). When group boundaries are so ill defined, it is very hard to say when Christianity separated from its mother religion.

METHODOLOGY

We will read each Gospel carefully, especially the first few chapters, again assuming that authors introduce important themes early in their works. In addition to thinking about each gospel's special themes, we will also compare their treatment of four common themes:

1. The messages of John the Baptist and of Jesus
2. The disciples and the early followers of Jesus
3. The description of gentile and Jewish concerns and issues
4. Jesus' final days, arrest, trial, and execution

We will see that some differences appear to be very small, sometimes only a couple of words. But changing a few words can affect the meaning of a passage very significantly. One example of this concerns Jesus' baptism.

When Jesus is baptized in the synoptic gospels, they report the words of a voice from heaven. In Mark, the voice says "*You* are my Son, the Beloved, with *you* I am well pleased" (Mk 1:11). In Matthew, the voice says "*This* is my Son, the Beloved, with *whom* I am well pleased" (Mt 3:17). Matthew copied Mark, but with a small change. He replaced the "you" to "this" or "whom." One might think this tiny change insignificant, but it is not. In Mark, the voice speaks to Jesus (and probably to Jesus alone), but Matthew makes it clear that the voice makes a public pronouncement: everyone around hears the voice and what it testifies about Jesus. This is a crucial thematic difference between Mark and Matthew, one that appears throughout their gospels.

The reason we have four canonical gospels is because the early church leaders, who determined which gospels (out of many gospels at their disposal) should be regarded as scripture, recognized that these four documents offered different arguments about Jesus. If the gospels all said exactly the same thing, the church would have selected only one gospel to include in the canon. Because of this, it is a disservice both to the gospel writers and to the tradition to gloss over and ignore differences, whether large or small.

CHAPTER 40

The Gospel of Mark

Read 1–4, 8–16.

In this chapter, we will:

- Study the oldest gospel, Mark, by reading it closely
- Examine Markan themes and his understanding of Jesus

We begin our exploration of the Gospels with Mark, because most scholars think it is the oldest gospel. One way of understanding Mark is to see him trying to explain the puzzle mentioned above: why do Jews not realize Jesus is the Son of God?

Markan Themes

Jesus' Ministry

   A. Who knew Jesus was God's Son?

       1. 1:11

       2. 1:24, 3:11

   B. Who does not?

       1. 3:19b-21

       2. 4:41

       3. 8:14–21

C. What does Jesus command people (or demons) to do when he cures (or exorcises) them? (See 1:40–45, 3:7–11, etc.) Do they obey?

D. Jesus taught in parables, according to Mark. But why does he do this, according to Mk 4:10–12?

*E. How public was Jesus' mission? How many people does Mark expect to hear and/or understand Jesus?

Disciples

A. The story in 8:22–26 is close to the midpoint of the book. Mark signals the importance of the story by making this miracle different all the others performed by Jesus: it takes him two attempts to heal the blind man. The story is a metaphor for the disciples. Summarize what happens in each verse:

v. 23

v. 24

v. 25a

v. 25b

A Metaphor for the Disciples?

A. How do the disciples understand Jesus before Chapter 8:22? Who do they think he is? (Review 4:41, 8:14–21.)

B. Immediately after the miracle, Jesus asks the disciples who he is. How do they respond?

C. The disciples were first century Galilean Jews. What did first century Jews expect of the Messiah? (See the historical introduction in Chapter 38.)

Passion Prediction 1

A. What will happen to the Son of Man, according to Jesus in Mk 8:31?

B. Why would Peter, a first century Galilean Jew, rebuke him (8:32)?

Passion Prediction 2

Jesus predicts the passion again in 9:30–31.

A. What is the response of the disciples in 9:32?

B. What was their response in 9:33–37? Why would they respond in this fashion?

Passion Prediction 3

Jesus predicts the passion again in 10:32–34.

A. What is the response of the disciples in 10:35–40?

B. How do the disciples' responses to Jesus' predictions of the passion relate to the healing of the blind man in Chapter 8? Where are they in the storyline of the miracle?

There is only one person in Mark who recognizes Jesus clearly. Look at Mk 15:39.

A. Who is the person? What is his religion?

B. What is his testimony?

C. Where does he fit into the miracle story in Chapter 8?

Mark's Thesis

Assume that by the time that Mark was writing, Jews were not flocking to join the followers of Jesus.

A. How do the pericopes you examined under the "Jesus' Ministry" heading explain it?

B. How do the pericopes you examined under the "Disciples" heading explain it?

Other Themes

We need to briefly consider our other themes.

John the Baptist and Jesus

   A. What is John's message according to Mk 1:4?

   B. What is Jesus' message in Mk 1:15?

Jesus' Final Days

Mark offers a rather odd portrait of the disciples and other followers of Jesus, especially since these were later revered as the founders of Christianity. Consider the following:

   A. What did Jesus ask the disciples to do in 14:32–42? What did they do?

   B. What did one of them do in 14:43–46?

   C. What did one of them do in 14:66–72?

   D. What did they do in 16:8?

16:8 is probably where the gospel ended originally, since verses 9–20 do not appear in the oldest Greek manuscripts of the New Testament. This abrupt ending has bothered Christians from the very early period, prompting them to write more satisfying (such as the so-called Shorter and Longer endings). But given Mark's general characterization of Jesus' followers, why would it be appropriate for his gospel to end in 16:8?

Jesus' Character

   A. Read 14:32–42. What was Jesus' prayer?

   B. Read 15:34. What was Jesus' question?

   C. How enthusiastic did Mark think Jesus was to be sacrificed?

Figure 40–1. The common method of burial for first century Jews was to entomb the deceased for a year or so on a ledge or bench. After their flesh had decayed, their bones were collected in an ossuary (a stone box for holding bones). The ossuary was then placed in a niche. This picture shows both the benches along the walls where bodies may have been laid and the niches to hold the ossuaries.

Jesus and Pilate. Read 15:1–15

A. What did Pilate charge Jesus with? (Notice that it is *not* a religious charge, such as blasphemy.)

B. How vigorous is Jesus' defense?

C. Other ancient sources (Josephus and Philo) describe Pilate as cruel and despotic. Is this how Mark portrays him in 15:6–15?

D. What does Jesus say when crucified? Is this consistent with Mark's earlier characterization of Jesus?

FOR FURTHER READING

Paul J. Achtemeier, "Mark, Gospel of," *Anchor Bible Dictionary (ABD)* 4:541–557.
Daniel R. Schwartz, "Pontius Pilate," *ABD* 5:395–401.

CHAPTER 41

Synoptic Gospels

In this chapter, we will:

- Study the so-called synoptic problem
- Think about a solution to the synoptic problem

The first three gospels are the *synoptic* gospels. *Synoptic* means "read together," and they received this label because from antiquity they were recognized as having significant literary and thematic similarities. To explore the relationship between these documents, fill out Table 41–01 as we read through Mark, Matthew, and Luke.

I have provided chapter and verse citations for Mark. You need to write brief descriptions of the verses for Mark. For Matthew and Luke, you will need to write their versions of the pericopes and note chapter and verse.

We will pay special attention to the first chapter of Mark and to the corresponding sections of Matthew and Luke.

Analysis

A. In which rows of Table 41–01 do all three sources report the same thing?

B. What does this suggest? How can you explain this?

C. In which rows do Matthew and Luke report something the same way, but which is omitted by Mark?

D. What does this suggest? How can you explain this?

TABLE 41-1 Synoptic Gospels Table

Pericope	Mark	Matthew	Luke
1. Genealogy		1:1-17	3:23-38
2. Pre-birth events and significance		1:18-25	1:5-24 1:26-39 1:39-56
3. Birth & infancy		2:1-12	2:1-20
4. Childhood		2:13-18	2:21-52
5. Reason for John the Baptist	1:2-3	3:3	3:3-6
6. John the Baptist's appearance	1:6	3:4	
7. John the Baptist's message	1:4b, 7-8	3:2	3:3b, 7b-14
8. John the Baptist's audience	1:5	3:5-7	3:7

TABLE 41–1 Synoptic Gospels Table *(continued)*

Pericope	Mark	Matthew	Luke
9. Jesus' baptism	1:9–11	3:13–17	3:21–22
10. Jesus' temptation	1:12–13	4:1–11	4:1–13
11. Jesus' first message	1:15	4:17	4:14–30
12. Jesus' disciples	1:16–20	4:18–22	5:1–11
13. Capern. synagogue	1:21–28		4:31–37
14. Healing	1:29–34		4:38–41
15. Galilee Tour	1:35–39	4:23–25	4:14–15
16. Healing of Leper	1:40–45	8:1–4	5:12–15

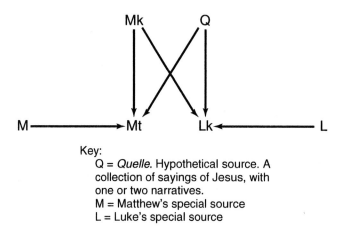

Key:
Q = *Quelle*. Hypothetical source. A collection of sayings of Jesus, with one or two narratives.
M = Matthew's special source
L = Luke's special source

Figure 41–1. This diagram illustrates the most common model to explain the patterns of agreement and disagreement between the different gospels.

E. In which rows do Mark and Matthew agree against Luke?

F. In which rows do Mark and Luke agree against Matthew?

Most scholars think Mark is the earliest gospel for a variety of reasons:

- It has the fewest number of pericopes, but individual pericopes are generally longer than those found in Matthew or Luke.
- Mark's Greek is generally not as compact and elegant as that of Matthew or Luke.

How does Figure 41–1 explain:

a. Why sometimes all the gospels say the same thing?

b. Why sometimes Matthew and Luke say the same think but Mark says nothing?

c. Why Mark and Matthew sometimes agree, but not Luke?

d. Why Mark and Luke sometimes agree, but not Matthew?

FOR FURTHER READING

C. M. Tuckett, "Synoptic Problem," *Anchor Bible Dictionary* (*ABD*) 6:263–70.
David L. Dungan, "Two-Gospel Hypothesis" *ABD* 6:671–79.

CHAPTER 42

The Gospel of Matthew

Read 1–5, 21–28.

In this chapter, we will:

- Examine Matthew's special themes
- Compare Matthew's description of Jesus' final days with that of Mark

Matthew is widely considered to have been written after Mark, largely because Matthew follows Mark's outline or sequence of events and uses Mark as a source. But Matthew must have thought Mark deficient or problematic, since he produced a different version of Jesus' life. (Again, as with Chronicles, why rewrite a history if it is perfectly acceptable and good?)

We will see that Matthew had a goal or thesis very different from Mark. In this chapter, we will explore how Matthew modified his source to produce his own gospel.

Matthew's Theme

The Genealogy

Matthew's major theme is apparent from the beginning of his gospel, which begins with a genealogy of Jesus. This seems an odd way to begin, especially since the genealogy traces Jesus' ancestry via Joseph, who had nothing to do with Jesus' conception (Mt 1:18, 20). Thus, this genealogy would seem to be irrelevant. But Matthew thought it significant enough to include and to begin his account of Jesus' life with. Why? What is he trying to accomplish or show? To answer these questions, read 1:17.

A. How long is it between significant events in Israel's history?

B. Who or what are identified as significant events?

    1. (first)

    2.

    3.

    4.

C. Who were these people important to? Whose history is being schematically re-counted here?

Visit of the Magi. Read 2:1–12.

In the ancient world, Babylonians (or Chaldeans) enjoyed a reputation for being skilled astrologers (see, for example, Dan 2:2).

A. Where were the magi from? Do you think they were diaspora Jews?

B. Who knew where the Messiah was supposed to be born?

C. Who went to pay homage to Jesus?

D. Where did they find Jesus?

E. How does this story condemn the Jewish elite?

Read the following passages: 1:22–23, 2:5–6, 2:15, 2:17–18, 2:23. All deal with Jesus' birth and nativity. What else do they have in common?

John the Baptist

Starting in Chapter 3, Matthew begins to include material from Mark.

A. What is John's message in 3:2?

B. Matthew adds 3:7–10 to John's speech. Who is singled out for special condemnation?

C. What is John talking about in these verses?

D. Compare Mk 1:7–8 to Mt 3:11–12. What has Matthew added?

Jesus' Biographical Model

The beginning of Matthew can be outlined in the following manner:

A. A baby is born in a miraculous fashion
B. Tyrannical king wanted to kill him (2:16)
C. Divine intervention allowed him to live safely in Egypt (2:13–15)
D. Exited from Egypt (2:19–20)
E. Passed through water (3:16–17)
F. Went up on mountain to reveal new Law (5:1, 17–48), which is described in five blocks (Ch 5–7, 10, 13, 18, 23–27)

*What character from the Old Testament has Matthew modeled Jesus upon?

Jesus and Torah

Read the Sermon on the Mount (Ch 5–7).
A. What is Jesus' attitude towards Jewish Law (5:17–20)?

B. How does he alter the law in 5:21–48? Does he make it easier or harder to observe?

In Matthew 23, Jesus condemns the scribes and the Pharisees.

C. What is the basis of his condemnation? Does he think they interpret Torah incorrectly?

Matthew's Goal or Thesis

A. What do your answers to the questions under "Genealogy," "Jesus and Torah," "Jesus' biographical model" have in common? Who would have been attracted to this version of Jesus' life and teachings?

B. Whom does Matthew condemn?

Other Themes

A. Matthew rejects several of Mark's themes. We saw that one of Mark's themes was non-recognition and secrecy. Matthew has a very different view. In the first three chapters, many people realize that Jesus is the Messiah. List at least three of them:

1.

2.

3.

B. Matthew presents the disciples in a very different light from Mark. Complete Table 42–1 to see some examples of revision.

TABLE 42–1

Mark	Event	Matt	Event
6:45–52		14:22–33	
8:27–30		16:13–20	
11:9–11		21:9–11	

How has Matthew changed Mark's description of the disciples?

John the Baptist and Jesus

We have already looked at the message of John the Baptist (above). But Matthew also presents the baptism differently. Read Mk 1:9–11 and Mt 3:13–17. Matthew introduces two major changes to Mk's account. What are they?

1.

2.

Matthew perhaps feared that readers might think that Jesus was spirtually inferior to John and/or was a disciple of John. We will see this is a perception that the other gospels address as well.

Compare Mk 15:1–15 to Mt 27:11–26.

A. Who is responsible for persuading the crowds to ask for Barabbas? How does this relate to Matthew's major theme?

B. What are the titles each gospel uses for Jesus? How are they appropriate in the context of the gospels?

Matthew is the only gospel to report the rite in 27:24. What is odd is that it is not a Roman custom, but rather one described in Deut. 21:6–7. He is also the only gospel to report the Jewish crowds' acceptance of the responsibility for the death of Jesus, the justification for much Christian anti-Semitic activity throughout history.

C. Matthew is the only gospel to report the stories in 27:62–66 and 28:11–15. Why do you think he includes them?

D. Matthew 28:1–10 follows Mark 16:1–8, but with changes.

1. What do the women do differently here?

2. Where are the disciples to go to await Jesus?

3. When Jesus meets the disciples, what message does he give them?

FOR FURTHER READING

John P. Meier, "Matthew, Gospel of," *Anchor Bible Dictionary* (*ABD*) 4:622–41.
Duane F. Watson, "Angels: New Testament," *ABD* 1:253–55.

CHAPTER 43

The Gospel of Luke

Read 1–6, 19–24.

In this chapter, we will:

- Investigate the themes of Luke
- Compare Luke's themes with those of Matthew and Mark

Luke's introduction (1:1–4) makes it clear that he was not an eyewitness to Jesus' ministry. Rather, he says he has studied the earlier accounts. They must be deficient (or else why rewrite the history?) and he suggests that his account will be "orderly" (1:3). As we will see, Luke also develops very different themes in his gospel from either Mark or Matthew.

Lukan Theme 1

Birth Narratives

Luke records a birth narrative for John the Baptist, the only gospel writer to do so. He also presents a birth narrative for Jesus (1:26–38, 2:1–20). Compare the birth narrative of Matthew (1:18–2:12) with that of Luke. List similarities and differences:

TABLE 43–1

Similarities	Differences

John the Baptist

We saw above that Matthew's description of John differed from Mark's, being changed to highlight his interests. Luke does the same thing. Read 3:7–20 carefully and compare it with Mk 1:5–9 and Mt 3:5–12.

A. Who did John address? Who is condemned? What might this suggest about his audience?

B. The crowd asked John questions. What was his advice (3:10–14)?

Jesus' Preaching

Matthew and Luke have Jesus emphasize different ideas in his preaching. To see this, compare the Beatitudes as reported by each of the authors.

TABLE 43–2

Matthew		Luke	
5:3		6:20	
5:6		6:21	

How are Jesus' sayings different in Luke?

The Audience for Jesus and God

A. What is the common theme in Lk 8:1–3, 10:38–41, 24:1–11?

B. Compare Mt 1:18–21 with Lk 1:26–35. How does Luke's story differ from Matthew's story?

* How do the answers you found for "Birth Narratives," "John the Baptist," "Jesus' Preaching," and "The Audience for Jesus and God" relate to social justice?

Lukan Theme 2

Genealogy

Luke's genealogy of Jesus is almost entirely different from Matthew's (look at who Joseph's father, grandfather, and great-grandfather were in each account). Luke's genealogy has a different purpose from Matthew's (notice that he doesn't try to divide it into sets of generations).

A. How far back did Matthew trace Jesus' genealogy?

B. How far back did Luke trace his genealogy?

C. Is Luke saying the same thing with his genealogy as Matthew? If not, what is Luke's reason for providing it?

Jesus' First Sermon

Luke describes Jesus' first public appearance as a sermon in Nazareth. He relocates and dramatically expands the account from Mark (Mk 6:1–6, Mt 13:53–58). What does he say that so angers the crowd that they try to lynch him? (See verses 26 and 27, especially.)

Based on the genealogy and the sermon on the mount, who is Luke's audience? How is it different from Matthew's audience?

Other Themes

We saw that Matthew changed the way the disciples were portrayed. Luke did likewise. Consider the following verses in Table 43–3:

TABLE 43–3

Mark		Luke	
8:27–33		9:18–22	
14:10–11		22:3–6	
14:32–42		22:39–46	

How has Luke changed Mark's description of the disciples?

Figure 43-1. All the gospels suggest that Jesus visited the temple and disrupted its functioning. This picture, of a model in Jerusalem's Holy Land Hotel, shows the temple (the tall structure in the center of the picture). Outside the temple was the court of the priests and the court of (male) Israelites, where people brought their sacrifices. East of the court of the Israelites was the court of the Israelite women (in the foreground). Outside these precincts was the court of the gentiles. Surrounding the court of the gentiles were porticos, which is probably where money changers worked and where birds and other sacrificial animals were sold to worshippers.

John the Baptist and Jesus

We already considered some of the changes Luke made to Mark's presentation of John, but Luke exhibits the same concern Matthew did regarding Jesus' baptism. Read Mk 1:9–11, Mt 3:13–17, and compare them with Lk 3:21–22. How is Luke's account different from the others?

Jesus' Final Days

JESUS' CHARACTER

A. Compare Mk 14:32–42 with Lk 22:39–46. What has Luke changed?

B. Compare Mk 15:21–24 with Lk 23:26–31. What has Luke changed?

C. Compare Mk 15:25–32 with Lk 23:35–43. What has Luke changed?

D. Compare Mk 15:34 with Lk 23:46. What has Luke changed?

* How does the character of Luke's Jesus differ from the description in Mark?

Jesus and Pilate

Compare Mk 15:1–15 and Lk 23:1–25.
A. What is Pilate's conclusion after questioning Jesus (23:4)? How is it different from Mk 15:4?

B. Luke is the only gospel to report the trial before Herod. Historians view this pericope with suspicion, since it violates Roman legal custom: Pilate would not have sent Jesus to Herod Antipas to be judged for crimes committed in Pilate's territory. Luke has Pilate report the outcome of the trial before Herod in 23:15. What is it?

C. Who does Luke think responsible for getting the crowd to demand the release of Barabbas?

D. Mk 15:10 parallels Lk 23:20. How has Luke changed his source?

E. Mk 15:14 parallels Lk 23:22. How has Luke changed his source?

F. Mk 15:39 parallels Lk 23:47. How has Luke changed his source?

* What is the conclusion that Luke wants the reader to draw from Jesus' trial and execution?

Post-Resurrection Appearances

Read Chapter 24.

A. Where were the disciples to remain after Jesus' death (verse 49)?

FOR FURTHER READING

Luke Timothy Johnson, "Luke—Acts, Book of," *Anchor Bible Dictionary* (*ABD*) 4:403–20.

CHAPTER 44

The Gospel of John

Read 1–5, 11, 18–21.

In this chapter, we will:

- Consider the only non-synoptic gospel and see how it differs from the synoptics
- Study John's very different account of Jesus' life and teachings

The synoptics each present Jesus differently. Mark emphasizes the suffering of Jesus, Matthew demonstrates Jesus' Jewishness, and Luke his innocence. But they agree on many other issues and events in Jesus' life: virgin birth in Bethlehem, baptism by John, which initiated public ministry, proclamation of the kingdom of God, teaching via parables, exorcisms, final supper, prayer in garden of Gethsemane. These are completely absent in John.

On the other hand, many of Jesus' most familiar sayings ("bread of life," "light of the world," "the way, the truth, and the life," etc.) and significant miracles (turning water into wine, resurrecting Lazarus, etc.) are reported in John and are not mentioned in the synoptics.

John's Christology

The Hymn

Christology means study of Christ. Different people conceived of Christ in different ways. Christology is the study of these different ways of understanding the importance of Christ.

Read 1:1–18. Many scholars think that vv 1–5,10–14, 16–18 were an early hymn to Jesus.

A. If this is true, verses 6–9 and 15 were inserted by John. What is the topic of these verses? How do they change the meaning of the hymn?

B. When did "the Word" come into existence?

C. When does John tell the reader who the Word is?

*This introduction is very different from that of the other gospels. How did John view Jesus differently than the synoptics?

Passover

A. What did John the Baptist call Jesus? (John is the only gospel writer to use this title and it is an important theme for John, first introduced in 1:29.)

B. The synoptics present the last supper as a seder supper (Mk 14:12–21), the ritual dinner celebrated by Jews at the first evening of Passover, when the pascal lambs were consumed, having been sacrificed earlier in the day. Jesus was arrested that night, tried the next day, and crucified the next afternoon. Read John 19:13–16.

   1. What day was it when Pilate sentenced Jesus to die?

   2. What time did Jesus die?

   *3. How does the title that John the Baptist gives to Jesus relate to John's shift in the crucifixion?

Other Themes: Jesus' Signs

John describes seven signs of Jesus:

1. 2:1–11 (water into wine)
2. 4:46–54 (healing the official's son)
3. 5:2–9 (healing a paralytic)
4. 6:1–14 (feeding 5,000)
5. 6:16–21 (walking on water)
6. 9:1–12 (healing a blind man)
7. 11:1–44 (raising Lazarus)

None of these stories is found in the synoptic gospels. In the synoptics, Jesus refused to do a "sign" (Mt 11:28). This is in line with the synoptic idea of a "secretive" Jesus. Let us think about why John presents Jesus doing signs.

Read 2:1–11

A. This story is mentioned in none of the other gospels. What is the point of the story?

B. Notice 2:11.

    1. Why is this incident significant in Jesus' life?

    2. Why is it significant for his disciples?

Read 4:46–54

A. What does John have Jesus tell the official?

B. Why is this incident significant, according to John?

Read Mk 5:21–43 and Jn 11:1–44

A. There are significant similarities between these stories. List at least three:

    1.

    2.

    3.

B. But there are important differences:

    1. Why does the person die in each story?

    2. How long is the person dead before being brought to back to life?

    3. Who witnesses the raising from the dead?

    4. Why does Jesus bring the victim back to life in each story?

C. What was the result of the sign in John?

D. Why does John recount the signs? What is his goal? (*Hint*: see 20:30–31.)

Jesus' Activities and Teaching

Reread Mk 4:1–34.

A. How did Jesus teach people, according to Mark?

B. Why did he use this method?

What did Jesus command the unclean spirits in Mk 1:25, 34, etc., and people he healed in Mk 1:43–44, 5:43, etc.?

Read John 5.

A. Jesus healed a paralytic (2–14). How is his command to him different than his command to people he healed in Mark?

B. John describes Jesus' teaching for most of the rest of the chapter (19–47). How is his teaching here different in format than in Mark?

C. How is it different in content? What is the subject of the teaching?

D. Skim through chapters 3 and 4. What is the subject of Jesus' teachings here?

Literary Elements

John exhibits some delightful literary elements, including relating various titles for Jesus to his miraculous activities. He also presents Jesus speaking with symbolic language, but his audience interprets it literally, giving Jesus the opportunity to explain and expound on the symbolic language.

A. After feeding 4,000 people (6:1–14), what is the title Jesus uses for himself in 6:35, 51?

B. What is the title Jesus uses for himself in 11:25? How does it relate to the story that follows immediately afterwards?

C. Examine the dialogue between Jesus and the Samaritan woman (John 4:7–15). What does Jesus offer the woman? What does she *think* he is offering her?

D. Examine the dialogue between Jesus and Nicodemus (John 3:3–7). What is Jesus talking about? What does Nicodemus *think* he is talking about?

Other Themes

Disciples (Read 1:35–51)

A. Review Mk 1:16–20. How did Jesus get his first disciples, according to Mark?

B. How does Jesus get his first disciples according to John?

John the Baptist (Read 1:19–34)

A. Compare 1:19–28 with Mk 1:2–8. How is John's description of John the Baptist similar to Mark's? How is it different?

B. How is John's description of Jesus' baptism different from Mark's in Mk 1:9–11?

C. Compare John's account of John the Baptist's message with that of Matthew (Mt 3:7–12). How is it different?

*We saw that Matthew and Luke were uncomfortable with the notion of Jesus being baptized by John, but they both quote his words predicting the Kingdom of God and the need to repent. What role does John the Baptist play in the gospel of John? Is his message similar?

Jesus' Final Days (Read John 18–19)

TRIAL

A. Review Mk 14:53–64. What did Jesus say to the council?

B. What did Jesus say before the high priest according to Jn (18:19–24)?

C. Compare Mk 15:1–15 with Jn 18:28–19:16. How does John's account differ?

1.

2.

3.

Review your answers on the Luke worksheet (Chapter 43) and compare them to the parallel passages in John. In each case, answer the question: "How does John's account differ from Mark's and Luke's?"

A. The trip to Golgotha (p. 224, question B) ‖ John 19:16b–18

B. The crucifixion (p. 224, question C) ‖ John 19:23–27

C. Jesus' death (p. 224, question D) ‖ John 19:28–30

FOR FURTHER READING

Robert Kysar, "John, Gospel of," *Anchor Bible Dictionary* (*ABD*) 3:912–31.

CHAPTER 45

Historical Jesus

In this chapter, we will:

- Consider the historiographical issues surrounding writing a biography of Jesus
- Examine some tools historians use when dealing with less than ideal sources

Before the Enlightenment, most Europeans lived lives that were not significantly different from those of the ancients, and their philosophical world-view (shaped by the Bible and classical literature) was similar to that of Jesus and his contemporaries. Since the Enlightenment, that has shifted. Hence, when we moderns read the gospels, we do so in a way very different from the way their authors intended, because we have a different world-view, expectations of histories, and biographies than the ancients.

One of the first things Biblical scholars did after the Enlightenment was to reconsider the descriptions of Jesus' life, found in the gospels, and try to re-interpret them in light of their new understanding of history. This is sometimes called the quest for the historical Jesus. Scholars comb the gospels, trying to identify nuggets of material acceptable to a modern, critical historian.

In this chapter, we will examine the problems facing a scholar trying to write a biography of Jesus and examine some of the tools that historians have developed to overcome these problems.

Miracles

For historians, supernatural (or miraculous) events are viewed with suspicion. Since historians try to establish plausible scenarios and not Truth (see Chapter 14), they are interested in the most *probable* explanation for an event. Most critical historians would say it is more probable that a disciple made up a story about Jesus walking on water than that Jesus did walk on water. They say this not because they are sacrilegious, but because it is *probable* that Christians made up stories about Jesus, and it is *improbable* (defying the laws of physics) for someone to walk on water.

We know that people make up stories all the time. When we discussed Mark, we noted that ending the gospel at Mk 16:8, while fitting into Mark's theme of disappointing disciples, made Christians uncomfortable enough to prompt them to write both the "Shorter" and "Longer" endings to the gospel.

Defying the laws of physics happens rarely (if ever) and usually prompts physicists to rewrite their laws to explain the unexpected phenomenon.

Modern discomfort with miracles has led some people to try to explain biblical miracles with naturalistic or scientific explanations. The crossing of the Red Sea (Ex 14) is explained in relation to winds and tides; quails naturally migrate across Sinai (Ex 16:13); and so forth.

We will not try to answer the question of whether miracles happen or not. It is enough for us to note that ancient people (and some moderns) thought they *did* happen. Historians may not be able to discuss whether miracles ocurr, but they can certainly discuss how miracles are recounted, how their descriptions change, and their significance for various authors and audiences.

Difficulties with the Sources

When writing history (reconstructing past events), historians need to use sources. Ideally, sources:

- Are numerous (so they can be compared)
- Derive from a time close to the event (to reduce the possibility that they are based on hearsay or legend)
- Are produced independently (independent witnesses make it more likely that an event happened)
- Do not contradict one another (which would imply that one or the other is in error)
- Are not biased toward the subject matter

*How well do the four gospels we have read thus far fulfill these ideals?

Historian's Tools

Historians try to overcome the limitations of their sources by using a variety of techniques to evaluate the reliability of various traditions. Three especially helpful ones are *independent attestation, dissimilarity,* and *contextual credibility.*

Independent Attestation

If several independent sources describe an event in the same way, it is more likely to be true. This does not deny that one source may be correct, but says that without corroborating evidence, there is no way to be sure that the author did not make up the event.

For writing a biography of the historical Jesus, there are several independent sources. Mark, Paul, Q, M (Matthew's source), and L (Luke's source). (Review your notes on the Synoptic Problem (Chapter 41) for more on these sources.)

One limitation for this criteria is that it can say *only* which traditions are more likely to be true. It cannot say which are not authentic.

Example: According to several sources (Mk 14:17–25, Jn 13, 1 Cor 11:23–26), Jesus ate a meal with his disciples shortly before his death. What was said and done at the meal may be historically suspect (see the next criterion, dissimilarity), but that there was a final supper is historically probable.

*What other stories that you think of that are multiply and independently attested?

Dissimilarity

Ancient sources were not unbiased in their reporting (recall the differing goals of the Deuteronomistic historian and the Chronicler and how their goals affected their treatment of David). Authors changed traditions (or even made up stories—remember the shorter and longer endings of Mark) to fit their goal, thesis, or bias.

For evaluating traditions about Jesus, the criterion of dissimilarity says that statements that agree with Christian views or ideology are historically suspect, because Christians made up stories that promoted their views. On the other hand, statements that disagree with Christian teachings or which reflect badly on Jesus or his followers would not have been made up by a Christian. Hence, they can be considered to be more historically probable.

Example: Early Christians thought Jesus was the Messiah. But he did not fit common Jewish expectations of what a messiah should be (see Chapter 38). Jesus was crucified like a common criminal. Since Jesus' death posed a problem for early Christians (recall how Mark's Jesus struggled to get his disciples to accept his new definition of "messiah"), it is unlikely they would have made up the story of the crucifixion. Hence it is historically likely to be true.

*What other incidents in the life of Jesus can you think of that satisfy the "dissimilarity" criteria?

Contextual Credibility

A tradition is more historically probable if it conforms to what is otherwise known about its historical context. If a saying or tradition about Jesus doesn't fit into what we know about first century Palestine and contemporary Jewish society, it is historically suspect.

Example: Some scholars have suggested that Jesus was influenced by the Greek philosophical school of the cynics. They point out that many of his teachings are similar to those of the cynics. Unfortunately, to other scholars, this idea doesn't meet the "contextual credibility" criteria. There is no evidence that Jesus knew Greek (he probably spoke Aramaic, like most first-century Galilean Jews). How he would have encountered cynic philosophers is also a problem, since there weren't many in Galilee!

*This is a difficult criterion for students who are not well versed in the societies of first century Palestine to evaluate. But review the "Jewish World-view" (Chapter 38) and try to think of examples of things said or done by Jesus that meet the "contextual credibility" criterion.

Based on your responses to the above three criteria, what can historians say about Jesus as a historical figure? (Note: This is not the same thing as Jesus as a theological figure. The affirmation that Jesus is the Messiah, the son of God, and the Redeemer is a statement of faith and relies on theological understandings, not historical assertions.)

FOR FURTHER READING

N. T. Wright, "Jesus: Quest for the Historical Jesus," *Anchor Bible Dictionary* (*ABD*) 3:796–802.

Non-Gospel
New Testament Materials

CHAPTER 46

Overview

In Part Four, we examined the gospel presentations of Jesus' life and teachings. We saw that each gospel writer presented Jesus in a different manner, depending on their understanding of who Jesus was, why Jesus was important, and what their goal was in writing about his life.

After examining the gospels, which present Jesus from a theological standpoint, we briefly considered the quest for the historical Jesus. What can modern historians say about Jesus from a *historic* rather than *theological* standpoint?

In Part Five, we will consider the other documents found in the New Testament. We do not have time to consider all the books of the New Testament (any more than we could consider every book in the Hebrew Bible), so we will focus our attention on three topics:

1. The history of the early church, as described in Acts
2. Paul, who spread Christianity geographically and ethnically
3. Revelation, the final book in the New Testament

We will concentrate on Paul, since the letters of Paul are the oldest documents in the New Testament. Moreover, Paul's importance for the development of Christianity is considerable. Paul is remembered by the Christian tradition for helping spread Christianity geographically and ethnically.

Paul preached about Jesus in a variety of geographic settings. Paul's initial mission, about which we know nothing, was in "Arabia" (Gal 1:17). Where, exactly, Paul went is unclear. After this, he traveled throughout Asia Minor (modern Turkey) and Greece, setting up churches. His final letter expressed his intent to visit Rome and to travel to Spain (Rom 15:23–24).

Additionally, where Jesus spoke to Jews, Paul saw himself as the "apostle to the gentiles." In his letters, he makes it clear that non-Jews were his main audience. Other apostles were sent to the "circumcised" (Gal 2:8), but Paul encouraged non-Jews to worship God and believe in Jesus.

We will consider the documents scholars agree are written by Paul before examining those which, although attributed to Paul, scholars suspect may have been written by someone else.

Finally, we will consider the book of Revelation, the second apocalypse found in the Bible. It concludes the New Testament, concludes the Bible, and will conclude this textbook.

CHAPTER 47

Acts

Read 1–5, 8:1–11:18, 15–18:17, 21–28.

In this chapter, we will:

- Consider the second book in Luke's description of early Christian history
- Study Luke's thesis and goal in writing his history

Acts is the second volume in Luke's history of early Christianity. How do we know this? Since Acts begins "In the first book, Theophilus . . .;" it is clear that Acts is the second volume in a history. Since the gospel of Luke is also dedicated to Theophilus (Lk 1:3), the two books must go together.

Beyond this rather obvious connection, we will see that there are many themes that connect Luke and Acts, themes which make it clear that Luke had a thesis about why Jesus' followers flourished and grew in numbers.

Common Themes in Luke and Acts

Geography

A. Luke signals the importance of geography early in his gospel. Where do the stories (found only in Luke) recounted in Lk 2:21–38 and 2:41–51 take place?

B. In Mark, Jesus leaves Galilee for Judea in 10:1 and enters Jerusalem in 11:1. In Luke, Jesus begins his journey in Lk 9:51 and enters Jerusalem in 19:29. Luke thus emphasizes Jesus' journey far more than does Mark.

C. How does Luke change Mark's description of Jesus cleansing the temple? Compare Mk 11:15–18 and Lk 19:45–48.

D. Finally, where are the disciples at the end of Luke's gospel (Lk 24:52–53) and what are they doing?

*What is the geographic progression in the gospel? What location(s) are important to Luke?

E. Read Acts 1:1–11. What does Jesus command the disciples to do?

F. Read Acts 1:8b. Luke presents the geographic spread of Christianity. Where are the disciples to preach?

   1.

   2.

   3.

Luke shows that this comes to pass throughout the book of Acts. Region 1 is the topic of Acts 1–7, region 2 is Acts 8:4–25, and region 3 is 8:26 to the end of the book.

History

A. Recall that in Mark, Jesus preaches about the Kingdom of God. When did he expect it? Look at Mk 1:15, 9:1, 13:30.

B. How is this different in Lk 11:20, 17:20–21?

C. Luke is very interested in history. He divides it into different periods in Lk 16:16. What are the periods?

   I

   Ia (transition to period II)

   II

A third period is described in Lk 24:46–47:

> IIa (end of period II)

> III

D. This theme appears early in Acts. The disciples want to know when the *parousia* (the return of Jesus) will occur (Acts 1:6). Jesus will not tell them, but tells them what to do while waiting in 1:8. What are they to do?

Parallel Patterns of Events in Luke and Acts

Mission

A. What initiated Jesus' mission? (See Lk 3:21–22, 4:14–15.)

B. What initiated the mission of the apostles? (See Acts 2:1–13.)

Reaction to Mission

A. What was the response to Jesus by Jewish leaders in Luke (22:1–2, 23:1–5, 10–13)?

B. What is their response in Acts 4:1–22, 5:17–42?

Jesus and Paul

According to Luke, Jesus' last days included trip to Jerusalem, where he was arrested; trial before Roman administrator; trial before Jewish leader; sentencing by Roman administrator; and death.

Skim the following and note (briefly) what happens in each section:

1. Acts 21:1–26

2. Acts 21:27–32

3. Acts 23:1–10

4. Acts 24:1–8

5. Acts 25:13–27

*What point is Luke making by presenting the parallel patterns of events? What (or who) is the model for the church?

Figure 47–1. According to Luke, Paul's preaching attracted so many people in Ephesos that sellers of statues of Artemis started a riot in its theater (Acts 19:23–41). A theater was first built in the Hellenistic period, but this photo shows it in its final form, dating to the reign of Trajan (98–117 CE). It could seat 24,000, which would have made for an impressive riot.

Common Themes within Acts

In addition to common themes between Luke and Acts, Luke developed common themes within Acts. Compare each of the following, noting who the actors are and what they do.

TABLE 47–1

Cite	Peter	Cite	Paul
3:11–26		13:16–18	
5:12–16		19:11–12	
12:6–11		16:23–40	
10:34–43		18:6–11	

Luke's Thesis

Is it merely coincidence that there is such a strongly parallel pattern between Luke and Acts and within Acts itself? Luke does not seem to have thought so. Rather, he presents it as the result of the Holy Spirit.

Interestingly, he seems to have thought of the Holy Spirit in at least two different ways.

A. Read the following verses from Acts. What does the Holy Spirit allow people to do?

  1. 1:8

  2. 2:4

  3. 4:8

B. Related to this are comments about the Hebrew Scriptures. What does the Holy Spirit do in the following verses?

  1. 1:16

  2. 4:25

  3. 28:25

C. But consider the following verses:

  1. 13:2, 4

  2. 15:28

  3. 16:6

*How are the last three references different from the previous six?

*How does the Holy Spirit explain the pattern of parallels observed in Luke and Acts?

FOR FURTHER READING

Luke Timothy Johnson, "Luke-Acts, Book of," *Anchor Bible Dictionary* 4:403–20.

CHAPTER 48

Paul's Life and Mission

Read Acts 9:1–31, 15:1–21, 22:3–21, 26:12–18; Galatians 1–2; Phil 3:1–11; 2 Cor 12:1–4.

In this chapter, we will:

- Consider Paul as a historical figure
- Compare the accounts about Paul found in Acts and Paul's letters

Paul was second only to Jesus in importance in the early Christian church. We will explore why Paul is so important on this worksheet and those that follow.

Paul is especially noteworthy because Luke reports his activities—he is the hero of the second half of Acts. But Paul's own writings have also been preserved and form the single largest block of New Testament documents (at least 13 of 27 documents claim Pauline authorship).

Before we turn to Paul's writings, we will consider Paul as a historical figure, much as we did Jesus in chapter 45. In this chapter, we will consider what we can say about Paul's biography from the two sources that discuss Paul in the New Testament: Paul's letters and Luke's Acts. We will divide Paul's life into three parts: (1) his life before his call to apostleship, (2) his call, and (3) his life as an apostle.

Life Before His Call

Read Gal 1.

A. What was Paul's attitude toward the church before conversion?

B. How did Paul characterize his life before his conversion?

Read Philippians 3.

  A. With which sect of Judaism did Paul affiliate?

  B. How did he characterize his life before his conversion?

      We cannot be sure of Paul's world-view *before* his call, since he does not reveal it. But it would be contextually credible for him to have a world view shared by other first century Jews. Look at the following verses, which (although written *after* his call) are similar to those of other first century Jews.

Read Rom 2:5–8; 1 Cor 7:26, 29b, 31b; 1 Thess 1:10, 4:17.

  A. What does Paul expect will happen in the future?

  B. When does he expect these things to come to pass?

  C. What sort of world-view is this?

Read Acts 22:3–21.

  A. What does Luke add to Paul's own description of his life before conversion?

  B. What was Paul doing when Jesus appeared to him?

  * Why do you think Paul persecuted the church before his conversion?

Paul's Call

Review Gal 1 and Phil 3.

  A. What does Paul say about his call?

  B. Where was Paul when God called him?

Read 2 Cor 12:1–4.

  A. How does Paul describe his vision here?

Read Acts 9.

   A. Where was Paul when called?

   B. What happened when Jesus appeared to Paul?

   C. What happened to Paul in Damascus?

   * Why do you think Paul's description of his call is so different from Luke's description of the same event?

Read Acts 23:1–10.

   On what ideas or beliefs did the Sadducees and Pharisees differ?

   * Paul and Luke both report that Paul was a Pharisee. What aspect of Pharisaic belief would have made Paul predisposed to believing that he did, indeed, see the risen Jesus?

Many scholars have commented on the continuity between Paul's beliefs before and after his call: he was a zealous, activist Pharisee who acted on his strong religious beliefs by attacking those who claimed Jesus was the Messiah. He probably shared the world-view of other first-century Jews. After his call, he was a zealous activist who had strong religious beliefs, but now professed Jesus to be the Messiah. Interestingly, his world-view need not have changed much to accommodate this. For this reason, it is important to see Paul in the context of first-century Judaism.

After the Call: Paul's Early Mission

Review Gal 1:16–24.

   A. What does Paul do immediately after seeing Jesus?

   B. Who did Paul confer with regarding Jesus and the gospel?

   C. How long was it before Paul went to Jerusalem to meet with the apostles?

   D. Who did Paul meet with and how long was he there?

E. Where did he go after his first visit to Jerusalem?

Read 2 Cor 11:32–33.

Where does Paul fit this famous story into his autobiography?

Review Acts 9:21–30.

A. Where did Paul go after his call?

B. How much time passed before Paul went to Jerusalem?

C. Who did he meet with in Jerusalem?

List the similarities and differences between Paul's account of his early mission and Luke's description of the same events.

TABLE 48–1

Similarities	Differences

THE APOSTOLIC CONFERENCE (REVIEW GAL 2:1–10.)

A. How long was it before Paul returned to Jerusalem?

B. How would you characterize Paul's attitude toward his opponents?

C. Who was to give the gospel to the gentiles (the uncircumcised)?

D. Who was to give it to the Jews (the circumcised)?

E. Who does Paul mention meeting in Jerusalem?

F. Who accompanied Paul to Jerusalem?

G. Why did Paul go to Jerusalem (i.e., who told him to go)?

Read Acts 15:1–22.

A. Why did Paul go to Jerusalem?

B. Who accompanied Paul to Jerusalem?

C. Who did Paul meet in Jerusalem?

D. Who was responsible for causing the debate about circumcision?

E. Who was supposed to spread the gospel to the gentiles?

F. How would you characterize the relationship between Peter and Paul, according to Luke?

Read Gal 2:11–14.

A. How would you characterize the relationship between Peter and Paul, according to Paul?

List some similarities and differences between the account of Paul's later missionary work, according to Paul and Luke.

TABLE 48–2

Similarities	Differences

*Look at the two lists of similarities and differences (Tables 48–1 and 48–2). Why do you think the two accounts (Luke and Paul) differed so much? Which do you think is more historically reliable?

FOR FURTHER READING

Hans Dieter Betz, "Apostle," Anchor Bible Dictionary (*ABD*) 1:309–11.
Charles B. Cousar, "Jerusalem, Council of," *ABD* 3:766–768.
Hans Dieter Betz, "Paul," *ABD* 5:186–201.

CHAPTER 49

Paul's Letters and Mission

Read 1 Thess, 2 Thess.

In this chapter, we will:

- Be introduced to Greco-Roman letter forms
- Think about why Paul wrote to Thessalonike
- Compare the different descriptions of Paul's missionary activity in Luke's and Paul's letters

The Form of Paul's Letters

When you write letters, you use different forms of letters for different audiences. A letter written for a job application will be very different from a letter written to your parents or a friend. Elements in letters are so ritualized that you can tell what sort of letter it is with very little inspection.

The same is true for ancient documents. Paul's letters seem odd to us in part because the Greco-Roman letter form is very different from our own. But his letters all have the same basic outline and are based on contemporary "private" letters. These letters have the following elements:

1. Salutation
   a. Sender's name (or, sometimes, a descriptive term)
   b. Recipient's name
   c. Greeting/well-wishing

All the elements of the salutation are conventions and should not be taken as necessarily reflecting the author's true feelings about the recipient. This is similar to the modern convention of starting letters with the term "Dear," even if you are writing to someone you do not know or may dislike.

2. Body of the letter
3. Words of encouragement, exhortation, greetings for other people
4. Closing prayer

Table 49–1 compares the structure of several of Paul's letters. Compare the chart and the above outline of typical Greco-Roman letters and note how Paul modified the form.[1]

TABLE 49–1

Element	1 Thess	1 Cor	2 Cor	Gal	Phil	Rom
1. Salutation						
A. Sender	1:1a	1:1	1:1a	1:1–2a	1:1	1:1–6
B. Recipient	1:1b	1:2	1:1b	1:2b	1:1	1:7a
C. Greeting	1:1c	1:3	1:2	1:3–5	1:2	1:7b
2. Thanksgiving	1:2–10 2:13 3:9–10	1:4–9	1:3–7	None	1:3–11	1:8–17
3. Body	2:1–3:8	1:10–4:21	1:8–9–9:14 10:1–13:10	1:6–4:31	1:12–2:11 3:1–4:1 4:10–20	1:18–11:36
4. Ethical exhortation and instructions	4:1–5:22	5:1–16:12 16:13–18	13:11a	5:1–6:15	2:12–29 4:2–6	12:1–15:13 15:14–32
5. Closing						
A. Peace wish	5:23–24	—	13:11b	6:16	4:7–9	15:33
B. Greetings	—	16:19–20a	13:13	—	4:21–22	16:1–15
C. Kiss	5:26	16:20b	13:12	—	—	16:16
D. Apostolic command	5:27	16:22	—	6:17	—	—
E. Benediction	5:28	16:23–24	13:14	6:18	4:23	16:20

* What has Paul added to the typical form of a private letter?

* Why did he make these changes to the typical letter? What was his goal?

As we read through the various letters, refer to this chart to help you discern their different parts.

Reasons for Paul's Letters

Another reason that Paul's letters are difficult to understand is that they are written in dialogue with his churches. With the exception of Romans, all of Paul's letters were written to churches that he founded. Paul was known to his churches and they were familiar to him. Thus, Paul does not present his basic theology or teachings in his letters—his audience would have known it already. Rather, he writes to his churches to address specific problems they are experiencing or to clarify questions his followers had about his earlier teaching.

---

[1]This chart is a simplified version of one found in C.J. Roetzel, *The Letters of Paul* (Atlanta: John Knox Press, 1982), 40.

Unfortunately, what these problems were is often unclear. The audience *knew* what the problems were, so Paul did not spend time reviewing them. Rather, he directs them on how to fix the problems. Thus, we hear only one side of the conversation. This is akin to being in a room listening to someone talking on a phone. You may be able to guess what the other person is saying (assuming the person in the room with you does more than grunt occasionally), but you cannot be sure your guesses are correct.

All of Paul's letters were written to address specific problems. One of the most important things to try to answer when reading Paul's letters is "What was the problem that prompted Paul to write this letter?" If you can figure out a reason or context for the letter, you will be able to understand the whole letter more fully.

Additionally, Paul can be loving and kind (as in 1 Thess), but at times is bitingly sarcastic and downright nasty (as in Gal). Several letters were prompted by his perception that interlopers were polluting his churches with different teachings. Especially with these sorts of letters, it is important to remember that Paul was not writing cool, objective descriptions, but engaged in strong, polemical argument. He was not trying to be factual or to depict his opponents in the way they might have described themselves, but wanted to convince his audience of the correctness of his positions. Do not assume that Paul's opponents would have agreed with Paul's presentation of their beliefs.

Paul's Mission

How did Paul spread the gospel of Jesus as Christ? We will compare the descriptions provided by Luke (in Acts) and Paul himself in 1 Thess, both discussing Paul's mission in Thessalonike.

The Chronology of Paul's Letters

The dates of Paul's letters are contested, but one possible chronology is as follows:[1]

1 Thessalonians	50–51 CE
2 Thessalonians	50–51, if authentic; last decades of first century if pseudonymous
Philippians	54–55
Philemon	54–55
Galatians	50–56
1 Corinthians	54
2 Corinthians	55–56
Romans	56–57
Colossians	57–61, if authentic; 70–90, if pseudonymous
Ephesians	85–90, assuming pseudonymity
1–2 Timothy	90–110, assuming pseudonymity
Titus	90–100, assuming pseudonymity

The dates for this chart are taken from the HarperCollins *Study Bible* (San Francisco: HarperCollins, 1993) 2113. For discussion of the chronological issues, see Hans Dieter Betz, "Paul," *ABD* 5:186–201.

Figure 49–1. One of the largest known disapora synagogues is at Sardis, northeast of Ephesus in Asia Minor. Many synagogues employed a basilica form, with a center aisle and two side aisles. At the end of the main aisle was an apse. In this photograph, the apse is the curved, marble-clad seating. In front of the apse is a very high table, perhaps for reading scripture. On the left side, you can see the remains of columns, which would have created the side aisles and supported the roof.

Read Acts 17:1–10a.

A. Where does Paul conduct his mission activity?

B. What is his message?

C. Who is his audience? Who believes his message?

D. Who are Paul's opponents?

Read 1 Thess 1:2–2:13, 17–20.

A. In 1 Thess 1:9–10, Paul refers to his message. What is his message? (See also 1 Cor 2:2.)

B. Who does Paul imply was his audience? (*Hint:* pay particular attention to 1:9; see also 1 Cor 12:2, Rom 1:5.)

C. Where did Paul proclaim his message?

D. How did Paul support himself in Thessalonike?

E. How did Paul characterize his activity in Thessalonike?

F. What might the last two points suggest about the socio-economic level of his audience?

* How do the descriptions from Paul and Luke differ?

* Which do you think is more *historically* reliable? Why?

Reason for the Letter

Read 1 Thess 3–5.

This is one of Paul's happiest letters. Why is he so euphoric about the Thessalonians?

Pay special attention to 4:13–5:11.

A. What event(s) in the church in Thessalonike prompted Paul to write this letter?

B. Why is this a problem? (*Hint:* See 1 Thess 1:10, 2:19b, 4:15b,)

C. How would you characterize Paul's worldview?

D. How does Paul address the problem?

2 Thessalonians

Read 2 Thessalonians. Some scholars think 2 Thessalonians was not written by Paul. The strongest evidence is the following.

A. How did Paul say the day of the Lord would come in 1 Thess 5:1–4?

B. When will it come, according to 2 Thess 2:2b–12?

    * Do these descriptions agree?

Forgery?

A. What does 2 Thess 2:2 suggest about forged letters?

B. What does 2 Thess 3:17 say?

C. If you look at Paul's other uncontested letters (Rom, 1 & 2 Cor, Gal, Phil, Phlm), how often does he indicate that he takes pen in hand to sign his letters?

    * Why might we think the author of 2 Thessalonians "doth protest too much"?

Reason for the Letter?

A. What does Paul condemn in Chapter 3?

B. What might prompt people to behave in such a manner? (*Hint:* Think about Paul's apocalyptic expectation.)

    * Assuming that 2 Thessalonians was not written by Paul, why do you think someone would forge a document under his name?

FOR FURTHER READING

Stanley K. Stowers, "Letters: Greek and Latin Letters," Anchor Bible Dictionary (*ABD*) 4:290–93.

Edgar M. Krentz, "Thessalonians, First and Second Epistles to the," ABD 6:515–23.

CHAPTER 50

Galatians and Corinthians

Read Galatians, 1 & 2 Corinthians.

In this chapter, we will:

- Consider the different understandings of what it meant to be a Christian in Paul's time
- Examine the divisions in the church in Corinth and Galatia
- Be introduced to several important Pauline metaphors and arguments

The dates for Paul's letters are difficult to establish. Most scholars agree 1 Thessalonians is the earliest, written ca. 50–51 CE, and that Romans (ca. 56–57 CE) is the latest. But the sequence and dating of the other letters is contested. We have already considered 1 and 2 Thessalonians and will look at Romans next. This chapter will consider three letters that are similar in that Paul deals with problems in churches he founded. We will consider Galatians first because the issues are perhaps easier to discern than in the letters to Corinth. Moreover, some of Paul's arguments in Galatians reappear in Romans.

Galatians

We have discussed 1 Thessalonians, perhaps Paul's happiest letter. Now we turn to Galatians, perhaps his angriest.

Angry?

A. Paul's exhibits his anger in the very form of his letter. Look at Table 49–1. What letter element is missing from Galatians?

B. Why is he so angry? What has prompted Paul to write this letter? (See 1:6.)

Paul's Argument

A. What is the "false" gospel?

   1. What did Paul and Cephas argue about (2:11–14)?

   2. Why is Abraham important to Paul (3:6–18)? (Review the "Abraham" chapter.)

   3. What activity does Paul condemn in 5:2–12? Why does he condemn it?

   *4. What can you say about the "false" gospel the Galatians followed?

B. How does Paul try to persuade the Galatians that *his* gospel is the correct one?

   1. What is Paul trying to accomplish in 1:11–2:10?

   2. What does Paul say about his gospel in Gal 1:1?

C. Redefinition of "Israel." Abraham is important for Paul (as noted above), but so are Abraham's wife and concubine. What is the point of his allegory about Sarah and Hagar (4:21–5:1)?

*D. Notice that Paul's discussion of Abraham quotes extensively from Torah (= Law). Why do you think he does this? What is he trying to accomplish?

1 Corinthians

Reasons for the Letter (See 1:10–17)

Fill out Table 50–1 on p. 261 to examine the different divisions in the church at Corinth.

* Can you discern a socio-economic pattern to these divisions? (*Hint:* pay particular attention to 1 and 3.)

TABLE 50–1

Citation	Division Based on . . .	Paul's Solution
1. 1:18–31		
2. 3:3–9		
3. 11:17–22		
4. 12:1–31		

These divisions were only part of the problem in Corinth. Fill out Table 50–2 to identify additional problems.

TABLE 50–2

Citation	Problem	Paul's Solution
1. 5:1–13		
2. 6:12–20		
3. 8:1–13		
4. 6:1–11		
5. 7:1–16		

Paul's Reasoning and Logic

A. In all the gospels, Jesus is a teacher. Notice how little Paul seems to know about Jesus. What does he say about Jesus in the following passages?

   1. 2:2

Figure 50–1. In this picture, you can see the remains of the Temple of Apollo at Corinth, which was about 600 years old by the time Paul visited. The hill behind and above the Temple of Apollo was the location of Corinth's acropolis. Corinth was sacked by the Romans in 146 BCE and re-founded as a Roman colony in 44 BCE. The Romans made significant changes to the Temple of Apollo and to the acropolis.

    2. 7:10–12, 25a

    3. 11:23–26

    4. 15:3–8

B. What is the source of Paul's world-view and philosophy, if not Jesus? What is discussed in these verses?

    1. 7:26–31

    2. 15:20–26

C. How would you describe Paul's world-view?

D. How does this world-view affect Paul's advice in 7:17–24, 26–28?

2 Corinthians

Tone of the Letter

A. Read the Thanksgiving section of this letter (1:3–7). How would you characterize Paul's tone?

B. Now read chapters 10–13 carefully. How would you characterize Paul's tone?

Structure of the Letter

A. What is the topic of 1 Cor 16:1–4? Where does it appear in the structure of the letter?

B. What is the theme of 2 Cor 9? Based on your answer to the previous question, where would you expect this in the structure of a Pauline letter?

* Some scholars argue that 2 Corinthians is comprised of (at least) two different letters that were combined by ancient scribes. Do you think the tone and structure of the letter supports this argument?

Paul's Opponents in Chapters 10–13

A. How do Paul's opponents criticize him? (See 10:10.)

B. How does Paul (sarcastically) describe his opponents (11:1–6)?

C. Based on Paul's comments in 11:21b–22, what can you say about his opponents?

*D. It has been suggested that Paul's opponents—the "super apostles"—might be advocating policies similar to those of his opponents in Galatia. Do you think this is possible? Why or why not?

A Summary of Paul's Relations with the Church in Corinth

The Corinthian correspondence is especially significant, as it is the only example where we can see Paul interacting with a church over a period of time. By carefully reading 1 and 2 Cor, we can discern the following sequence of visits and letters:

1. First visit—Established church, gained initial converts
2. Paul's first letter—Mentioned in 1 Cor 5:9 but not extant
3. Corinthians' first letter to Paul (mentioned in 1 Cor 7:1)

4. Paul's second letter—1 Corinthians—written in response to report from Chloe's people (1:11) and letter from Corinthians (7:1)
5. Paul's second visit was painful visit (2 Cor 2:1–4). Paul not well received and embarrassed or irritated by member of congregation (2:5–11)
6. Arrival of super apostles in Corinth
7. Paul's third letter (2 Cor 10–13) was one he later labeled the "painful" letter (2 Cor 2:4).
8. Paul's fourth letter—conciliatory letter (2 Cor 1–9)

FOR FURTHER READING

Hans Dieter Betz, "Galatians, Epistle to the," *Anchor Bible Dictionary* (*ABD*) 2:872–75.

Hans Dieter Betz and Margaret M. Mitchell, "Corinthians, First Epistle to the," *ABD* 1:1139–1148.

Hans Dieter Betz, "Corinthians, Second Epistle to," *ABD* 1:1148–54.

CHAPTER 51

Romans

Read Romans.

In this chapter, we will:

- Try to understand elements of Paul's theology

Romans is the only letter written by Paul to a church that he did not found. It is of great interest to historians and theologians because it contains the fullest description of Paul's theology and ideas concerning the Law, faith, and salvation. Before we turn to these issues, we will briefly consider the reason (or occasion) for the letter.

Reason for Letter

*A. Based on Paul's letters, especially 2 Cor 10–13 and Galatians, what sort of reputation do you think Paul had? What would the people in the church in Rome have heard about him?

B. Read 16:1–16. Why do you think Paul addresses so many people? What is his goal? How does this address the "reputation" issue?

C. Read 15:22–29. Why is Paul writing to the church in Rome?

Since Paul did not start the church in Rome, he needs to explain his gospel and theology to them in his letter. This is especially important because the early Christians were working out their theology about Jesus and there was lots of disagreement about many issues. Paul provides a synopsis of his argument in 1:16–17.

a. "I am not ashamed of the gospel." Paul, as we saw in Galatians, asserts there is only one gospel (his own), but it is clear that other Christians offered different interpretations. Paul announces his intention to stand by, explain, and, perhaps, defend his gospel.

b. "It is the power of God for salvation. . ."

c. "Salvation for everyone who has faith. . ."

d. "To the Jew first and also to the Greek. . ."

e. "For in it the righteousness of God is revealed through faith for faith."

We will explore these issues in some detail below.

Paul on the Human Condition (Romans 1:18–3:20)

Paul begins his argument by defining "salvation." He knew that everyone dies and saw this as God's punishment for not living in accord with God's instructions (or Torah or Law).

A. But is it fair for God to punish gentiles, who did not know Torah? What is Paul's response to this objection in 1:18–2:16?

B. Since Jews have Torah, why are they punished? How does Paul explain this in 2:17–3:20?

Not living in accord with God's instructions is *sin* and is punished by *death*. Salvation delivers one from sin and death. Paul explores the source of salvation, starting in Rom 3:21.

A. Can one be saved by obedience and good behavior? (See 3:21a, 23.)

B. People never escape sin, so how can they avoid the punishment of death? (See 3:24b, 25a.)

C. How can people gain redemption? (See 3:26b, 28.) Notice that Paul does not suggest that people *become* unsinful, only that they will be treated *as if* they were unsinful!

Paul supports his argument by reference to Abraham, returning to an example we saw earlier in Galatians.

A. How does Abraham support his argument that people are justified by faith? (See 4:3.)

B. But God ordered Abraham to circumcise himself, so why shouldn't contemporary believers? How does Paul answer this in 4:9–11?

Salvation

How does Jesus' death *cause* salvation? Paul offers two different models or metaphors to explain the mystery of salvation to his audience. Unfortunately, he uses the same terms (sin, death, justification, etc.) for the two models. He also does not clearly differentiate between them. This makes it hard to understand them, but doing so clarifies Paul's argument.

The Judicial Model (Read 5:1–21)

A. Paul starts explaining that death is caused by sin. How did sin come into the world?

B. Who pays for the transgression of Adam?

C. Jesus' willing sacrifice (5:6, 8) is a gift. How does it affect humanity's relationship to God (see 5:17b, 18b, 19b)?

In short, if people have faith in Jesus, God, the judge, will consider them to be righteous (i.e., in the right or sinless), *even though* they continue to be sinful.

The Participatory Model (Read 6:1–14)

A. How does Paul characterize sin and death in these verses (see 6:1, 10, 11, 12, 14)? Is it the same as in the judicial model?

B. Why does Paul think baptism is significant? Look at verses 3 and 4.

C. Does baptism ensure that one is saved and living in the Kingdom of God? Look at verses 5b, 8b.

Notice that Paul does not suggest that baptism will guarantee salvation: one must behave properly afterwards too. How Christians should behave is the focus of his discussion from 6:15–8:39. His basic point is that, although free from law, people cannot behave in a lawless and sinful fashion. Rather, their life should reflect the fact that the Spirit now dwells in them and offers them hope for a glorious future (8:18–30).

You may recall that Paul offered similar advice in other places (1 Cor 6:12ff, 2 Cor 12:11–13).

Jews and Greeks

The next topic in Paul's synopsis is "To the Jew first and also to the Greek." He spends several chapters (Rom 9–11) addressing the question "Hasn't God reneged on his promises to Abraham and the other patriarchs, that the Jews will receive preferential treatment from God?"

A. How does he refute this argument in 9:6–15? He offers a similar refutation in Gal 4:21–31.

B. How does he refute this argument in 9:19–29?

C. What is Paul's warning in 11:13–24? What could have prompted this warning?

D. Is Paul optimistic about the fate of the Jews? Read 11:25–36?

In the final few chapters, Paul offers ethical exhortations to the Romans to live their lives in appropriate fashion for Christians.

FOR FURTHER READING

Charles D. Myers, Jr. "Romans, Epistle to the," *Anchor Bible Dictionary (ABD)* 5:816–830.

Hans Dieter Betz, "Paul," *ABD* 5:186–201

CHAPTER 52

The Acts of Paul and Thekla

In this chapter, we will:

- Consider one example of an ancient Christian document that was not accepted into the scriptural canon
- Think about the formation of canon and what criteria was used to determine what was scripture

It may come as a surprise, but "scripture" for Jesus and his immediate followers, including Paul, meant the Hebrew Bible (or, more precisely, the Septuagint). But people who believed Jesus was the Messiah produced lots of literature, some of which was accepted by later church leaders as scripture. The material found in our New Testament represents only a small sample of this larger body of literature. Some of it sounds very weird to us today:

- The Gospel of Peter says Herod ordered Jesus' crucifixion. Later, a crowd saw three people, whose heads reached up to the clouds, come out of Jesus' tomb, followed by a cross, which had a dialogue with a voice from heaven.
- The Infancy Gospel of Thomas describes Jesus' activities as a youngster. These include causing other children and even his teacher to fall down dead, although he later revives them.
- The Gospel of Thomas is a collection of sayings attributed to Jesus. Some are similar to those in the Synoptics, but others seem to suggest that Jesus revealed special knowledge (*gnosis*) to his followers that was necessary for salvation.

The catalyst to create a Christian canon may have been provided by Marcion, an early second century Christian. Marcion thought the God of the Hebrew Bible was evil and had nothing to do with Jesus, who was sent by the true God. Since Marcion could not use the Hebrew Bible, he needed to create scripture for his churches. He did so by collecting the letters of Paul and combining them with an edited version of the gospel attributed to Luke.

Other Christians responded by creating the core of the present New Testament. They, too, took Paul's letters, but they added the four gospels (Mt, Mk, Lk, Jn) they thought were the most ancient to create the canon. What other documents should be accepted into the canon as scripture? The status of Hebrews, Revelation, and 1 Clement remained unclear for centuries. It was not until 367 CE that a Christian author identified all the books found in the current New Testament as scripture!

The text we will be exploring in this chapter is an example of early Christian literature, but the early church did not regard it as scripture. We will consider why this might be at the end of this worksheet.

Read "The Acts of Paul and Thekla" (appendix, pp. 298–303) and answer the following questions.

Characterization of Paul

A. How is Paul described physically?

B. What does Paul do when Thekla is on trial and being punished in Iconium?

C. What does Paul do when Thekla is accosted in Antioch?

D. What does Paul do when Thekla is on trial and being punished in Antioch?

E. What is the significance of Paul's traveling companions, Demas and Ermogenes?

Characterization of Thekla

A. What does the author say about Thekla when she is first introduced?

B. What does Thekla do when Paul is imprisoned in Iconium?

C. What does Thekla do when she is to be burned alive?

D. What does she do when she is accosted in Antioch?

E. What does she do when she is given to the wild beasts?

Paul's Teaching

A. What are the main points of the teaching of "Paul" in paragraph 3?

B. Review 1 Cor 7. Does this passage agree with *The Acts of Paul and Thekla?*

* Do you think the author of *Paul and Thekla* was familiar with the writings of Paul? Why or why not?

Gender Issues

A. Who vocally support Thekla in Antioch? (See paragraphs 17, 20, 21, 23, etc.)

B. Who organize the attacks on her in Iconium and Antioch?

C. Who forms the core of Paul's audience in Iconium?

D. Notice that the presence of women in Paul's churches is documented in several places (see the next chapter) in Paul's letters.

1. Read Romans 16. What is the office held by Junia?

2. How many other women are listed here?

3. Who notifies him of problems in the church at Corinth (1 Cor 1:11)?

E. Who is the hero of this story?

*F. Why do you think Paul's message (in this story) was so appealing to Thekla and the other women of Iconium?

Non-Canonical Status

There was a variety of different gospels in circulation, but the church chose to declare only Matthew, Mark, Luke, and John scriptural. There was also a variety of stories about Paul, including this one, but the church declared only Acts scriptural.

Tertullian, a leader in the church from North Africa, said that the Acts of Paul and Thekla was composed in Asia Minor "from a love of Paul." Since it was recognized as a forgery, it was rejected from the canon.

* There are other documents that were pseudonymous (see the next chapter), which the church accepted into the canon. What about the Acts of Paul and Thekla might have encouraged the church to recognize it as pseudonymous?

FOR FURTHER READING

John J. Clabeaux, "Marcion," *Anchor Bible Dictionary* (*ABD*) 4:514–516.
Dennis R. MacDonald, "Thekla, Acts of," *ABD* 6:443–444.

CHAPTER 53

Deutero-Pauline Literature

Read 1 Tim, Titus, Ephesians.

In this chapter, we will:

- Examine letters attributed to Paul, but which may have been written by someone in Paul's name
- Think about the different attitudes Paul had toward a variety of issues from those expressed in later church teaching

Although thirteen books in the New Testament claim to be written by Paul, only seven (Rom, 1 Cor, 2 Cor, Gal, Phil, 1 Thess, Phlm) do scholars universally agree were written by Paul. The other six fall into two groups: the Deutero-Pauline and the Pastoral epistles.

Scholars debate whether the Deutero-Pauline documents (Eph, Col, 2 Thess) were written by Paul. The Pastoral epistles (1 Tim, 2 Tim, Titus), on the other hand, are widely regarded by scholars as deriving from someone other than Paul, for many reasons.

Some of the best reasons to doubt Pauline authorship relates to the style of writing. The uncontested letters use relatively short and simple sentences, but the contested letters have much longer and more complex sentences. This is not apparent in English translations, since translators chop up very long Greek sentences into shorter sentences in English. Additionally, the Pastorals and the Deutero-Pauline letters use many words not found in the uncontested Pauline corpus. And when they do use the same words, frequently they use them differently than Paul did. Unfortunately, these stylistic criteria cannot be evaluated without learning Greek, so we will not dwell on them.

Rather, in this worksheet, we will examine reasons scholars doubt Pauline authorship, focusing on those elements that can be discerned in English translations.

Attitudes toward Women

Leadership

A. Read Romans 16. What titles or offices does Paul give to the following people?

> Phoebe (v. 1)

> Prisca (v. 3)

> Junia (v. 7)

> Tryphæna (v. 12)

> Tryphosa (v. 12)

All these individuals are women.

B. Read 1 Timothy. The "Pastor" offers several directions regarding women in 2:9–15. List them:

> v. 9

> v. 11

> v. 12

*C. Why might scholars suspect that 1 Tim 2 and Romans 16 were written by different people?

Salvation

A. Review the "Romans" worksheet. What are the two models Paul uses to explain salvation?

B. What do people need to do to be saved?

C. Read Gal 3:28. Paul identifies three pairs of "opposites." List them:

1.

2.

3.

*What is Paul's basic point with Gal 3:28?

    D. Read 1 Tim 2:15. How are women to achieve salvation?

*E. Why might scholars doubt the same person wrote Romans and Galatians as wrote 1 Tim?

Widows

    A. Read 1 Cor 7:8–9, 25–31.

        1. What advice does Paul give widowers and widows?

        2. What advice does Paul give virgins?

    B. Read 1 Tim 5:14–16 (and review 1 Tim 2:15). What advice does the Pastor give (young) widows?

*C. Why might scholars doubt the same person wrote these passages?

Christian household

    A. Wives and husbands

        1. Read 1 Cor 7:1–6. How does Paul characterize the relationship between husband and wife here?

        2. Read Eph 5:21–32. How does this author characterize the relationship between husband and wife?

     *3. Why might scholars doubt the same person wrote these two passages?

    B. Slaves and masters

        1. Read Eph 6:5–9. How does the author characterize the master–slave relationship?

        2. Read Titus 2. How is this passage different from Eph 6:5–9?

Notice that even within the Deutero-Pauline literature, there are shifts in attitudes toward slaves.

Church Organization

Read 1 Cor 12:7–11, 27–31; 14:26–33, 37–40.

[Note: many scholars think 14:34–36 were added to Paul's letter, perhaps in the 2nd century, to get it to agree with the Pastorals. These verses seem to interrupt the flow of Paul's thought—if you skip these verses, Paul's writing flows quite smoothly.]

   A. Who determines who should speak in church?

   B. How does Paul rank spiritual gifts?

   C. What are the offices in his churches? What are the qualifications for the different offices?

Read 1 Tim 3:2–13, 5:3–13.

   A. What are the requirements for *bishop?*

   B. What are the requirements for *deacon?*

   C. What are the requirements for *widow?*

   * What is different about the organizational structure reflected in 1 Cor and 1 Tim?

Other Issues

Prior Life

   A. Read Phil 3:4b–6. How does Paul characterize his life before his call?

   B. Read 1 Cor 4:4. How does Paul characterize his life before his call here?

   C. Read Titus 3:3. How does this author describe pre-Christian life?

   D. Read Eph 2:3. How does this author describe pre-Christian life?

*E. Why might scholars doubt the same person wrote these various passages?

Some people think that scholars who suggest that Paul did not write all the letters attributed to him are trying to denigrate the New Testament. And it is easy, perhaps, to understand this argument.

* However, some believers might find it empowering to separate the Pastorals from the undisputed Pauline letters. Can you think of groups might like to do this?

FOR FURTHER READING

Jerome D. Quinn, "Timothy and Titus, Epistles to," *Anchor Bible Dictionary* (*ABD*) 6:560–71.
Elisabeth Schüssler Fiorenza, "Feminist Hermeneutics," *ABD* 2:783–91.

CHAPTER 54

Revelation

Read Isa 6:1–8, Ezek 1, Dan 7, Rev 1–6, 12–13, 20–22.

In this chapter, we will:

- Examine the second apocalypse in the Bible
- Study Revelation in relation to its Hebrew Bible predecessors

Revelation is last book in the New Testament canon. It was also the book the church debated about longest before including it in the canon. The relish with which John of Patmos, the author of Revelation, describes the torment of people by agents of God, does not seem to be in accord with other teachings of the New Testament or the church's understanding of what it meant to be a Christian. (Consider Chapter 9:1–6, which describes stinging locusts who "were allowed to torture them for five months, but not to kill them. . . In those days, people will seek death but will not find it; they will long to die, but death will flee from them.")

Revelation is an apocalypse, a genre of literature that was popular among Jews from 200 BCE to 100 CE and also among the early Christians. Both these groups, as we have seen, had an apocalyptic world-view (see Chapter 38) and an apocalypse is the literary expression of this world-view. We saw an example of an early apocalypse when we read Daniel (Chapter 37).

Revelation differs in a variety of ways from other apocalypses. First, its literary form is odd. After an introduction (Rev 1), it has letters to seven churches in Asia (Rev 2–3). Its conclusion (22:1–21) also uses elements of an epistle. But chapters 4–22 describe John's vision(s) of heaven and the future. So is Revelation an epistle or something else?

Second, most apocalypses are pseudonymous. The author claims to be someone else, usually someone famous from the Hebrew Bible. There are apocalypses attributed to Enoch, Ezekiel, Ezra, Baruch, Adam, Elijah, and others. When we read Daniel, we saw there were reasons to doubt that it was written by a 6 century BCE visionary in the Babylonian court. But the author of Revelation claims no special status: he is John of Patmos (1:9). Later Christians may have associated him with the author of the gospel of John, but their Greek is different enough that most modern scholars reject this association.

Third, because apocalypses reveal divine or secret knowledge, most contain a command that they be kept secret. "But you, Daniel, keep the words secret and the book sealed until the time of the end" (Dan 12:4). Revelation contains the opposite command: "Do not seal up the words of the prophecy of this book, for the time is near" (Rev 22:10). This feature may be related to pseudonymity. Secrecy was a way to explain why documents written by Adam, Enoch, Elijah, and other ancient worthies suddenly appeared.

We will examine a variety of typical apocalyptic elements in Revelation: tours of heaven, use of ancient mythic language, and symbolic language. Before we get to these, however, we will consider the historical importance of the seven letters.

Early Christian Communities

Revelation begins (chapters 1–3) with letters to seven churches in Asia. We previously saw that Luke describes the early Christian movement as harmonious. People lived communally, and theological debates or differences were settled by meetings (Acts 15). Paul's letters presented a very different picture: he got into heated debates with people who advocated different gospels. An especially difficult topic was whether gentiles needed to observe (some) Jewish practices. Similarly, the author of the Pastoral letters attempts to correct what he sees as improper behavior in Christian churches.

Figure 54–1. John refers to Pergamum as where Satan's throne is located (Rev 2:13). In this photo, you can see the amazing location of Pergamum's acropolis. On the side of the hill was an impressive theater and above it was the famous Zeus Altar (now located in Berlin). The crane is reconstructing a temple to the imperial cult.

Which model—the Holy Spirit harmoniously guiding the church or humans struggling to understand what it means to follow Jesus—does Revelation support? Read chapters 2–3.

Opponents

A. Who does John condemn in Ephesus?

B. Where else does he condemn these people?

Names of Opponents

A. What names from the Hebrew Bible does he attach to his opponents?

B. Are these positive names? Do you think these were names the opponents choose for themselves?

*C. Are these opponents from outside the Christian movement?

Other Opponents

A. Who does John condemn in Smyrna and Philadelphia?

*B. Are these opponents from outside the Christian movement?

*C. Which model of early Christian history do John's letters support?

Tours of Heaven

When we read Ezekiel, we saw that he struggled to describe, using human language, his vision of the divine. John also struggled with the limitations of human language and fell back on metaphors or images found in the Hebrew Bible. What was John's inspiration for each of the following verses?

A. 4:2

B. 4:4

C. 4:6b–7

D. 4:8

Cycles of Destruction

After the vision of God's heavenly throne, John describes the first of three cycles of destruction of the world. In the first cycle, some disaster happens when each of seven seals of a scroll are opened (Rev 6). What happens when each seal is opened?

A. First seal:

B. Second seal:

C. Third seal:

D. Fourth seal:

* What is the common theme of the first four seals?

E. Fifth seal:

* With the fifth seal, John reveals the reason for destruction of the world. What is it?

F. Sixth seal:

* What remains in the world after the sixth seal is opened?

When the seventh seal is opened (8:1), another cycle of seven disasters is described (chapters 8 and 9). These disasters occur when angels blow trumpets. Later in the book (chapters 15 and 16), a third cycle of disasters is described, initiated when angels pour out bowl of the wrath of God upon the earth.

Recrudescence of Ancient Mythic Material

One common feature of apocalyptic literature is that it makes references to very archaic material. Read Chapter 12.

A. Who battles whom in 12:1–9?

B. Review Chapter 2 of this textbook. What does God battle in Psalms?

C. How does John identify the dragon in Chapter 12?

D. What happens to the dragon (and his angels) after being tossed out of heaven?

* How is John's description of the battle different from the ancient material found in Psalms (Review Chapter 2)?

Symbolic Language

Apocalyptic literature employs a rich symbolic language. Some of these symbols are fairly straightforward and intelligible, but others are (to modern readers, anyway) virtually incomprehensible. As with his descriptions of the heavenly court, John borrows some of this symbolic language from the Hebrew Bible.

A. What similarities can you find between Revelation 13 and Daniel 7?

Gematriya

Ancient Hebrew and Greek did not have a separate number system (as we use Arabic numerals). Rather, they assigned numeric values to the letters in the alphabet. In English, this would be done as follows:

A = 1, B = 2, C = 3, D = 4, E = 5, F = 6, G = 7, H = 8, I = 9, J = 10, K = 20, L = 30, M = 40. . . T = 100, U = 200, V = 300, etc.

Because of this, each word could be assigned a numerical value. This is called, in Hebrew, gematriya.

"Number of the Beast" is either 666 or 616 (depending on the text). Using gematriya with the Greek letters of the name "Nero" is 616 and its variant spelling, "Neron", is 666. For this reason, many scholars think John was referring to the Emperor Nero in a veiled manner in 13:18.

B. In verse 13:7b, John gives a clue as to who the beast represents. In John's time, who was given "authority over every tribe and people and language and nation"?

Symbols can mean different things simultaneously. John returns to the beast in chapter 17, but now it supports a woman, "the mother of whores."

A. What is the name John gives the "mother of whores"?

B. What is the significance of this name? What is it associated with in the Hebrew Bible?

C. Does John use the metaphor of "whoredom" the same way it was used by the prophets we studied earlier (see Chapters 29 and 30)?

D. The woman represents a city. Which city does John mean? (*Hint:* John provides a clue to the identification of the city in 17:9.)

John describes the fall of Babylon in Rev 18, which evokes rejoicing in heaven, described in Rev 19. Chapters 20–22 have periodically prompted much excitement among believers, since they predict the final defeat of Satan, in graphic language.

In a certain respect, all the battles and destruction are leading up to chapter 21, which describes "a new heaven and a new earth" (Rev 21:1).

A. Who has no place in the new creation?

B. What are the dimensions of the new Jerusalem?

C. Where are its gates located?

D. What is it constructed out of?

E. How is it illuminated?

F. What vegetation is found in it? Where have we seen this vegetation previously?

* How is the new Jerusalem different than the old Jerusalem? What is John trying to emphasize in this description?

John's Goal or Purpose

We noted above that Revelation made the early church leaders uncomfortable, but this was not John's goal.

A. What was happening to his audience? Look at Rev 2:3, 9–10, 13, 3:10.

B. What reason did John provide for the death and destruction when the fifth seal was opened?

C. Who survives and enters into the new creation?

* What is John's reason or goal for writing to the churches?

FOR FURTHER READING

Adela Yarbro Collins, "Revelation, Book of," *Anchor Bible Dictionary* (*ABD*) 5:694–708.
Adela Yarbro Collins, "Apocalypses and Apocalypticism: Early Christian," *ABD* 1:288–292.

APPENDIX

Ancient Primary Source Material

ENEUMA ELIS

The date of this Creation Story from Mesopotamia is debated. It certainly existed by 1125 BCE and was probably composed between 1800 and 1200 BCE. The story was well known and in circulation until about 500 CE.[1]

Tablet I

1. When in the height heaven was not named,
2. And the earth beneath did not yet bear a name,
3. And the primeval Apsû, who begat them,
4. And chaos, Tiamat, the mother of them both,—
5. Their waters were mingled together,
6. And no field was formed, no marsh was to be seen;
7. When of the gods none had been called into being,
8. And none bore a name, and no destinies [were ordained];
9. Then were created the gods in the midst of [heaven],
10. Lahmu and Lahamu were called into being [. . .].
11. Ages increased, [. . .],
12. Then Anshar and Kishar were created, and over them [. . .].

13. Long were the days, then there came forth [. . .]
14. Anu, their son, [. . .]
15. Anshar and Anu [. . .]
16. And the god Anu [. . .]
17. Nudimmud, whom his fathers [his] begetters [. . .]
18. Abounding in all wisdom, [. . .]
19. He was exceeding strong [. . .]
20. He had no rival [. . .]
21. (Thus) were established and [were . . . the great gods (?)]. . . . .
22. Apsû opened his mouth [and spake],
23. And unto Tiamat, the glistening one, he addressed [the word]:
24. "[. . .] their way [. . .],
25. "By day I cannot rest, by night [I cannot lie down (in peace)].
26. "But I will destroy their way, I will [. . .],

[1]This text is from L. W. King, *The Seven Tablets of Creation* (1902), available at http://www.sacred-texts.com/ane/stc/index.htm. I have abridged the text.

27. "Let there be lamentation, and let us lie down (again in peace)."
28. When Tiamat [heard] these words,
29. She raged and cried aloud [. . .].
30. [She . . .] grievously [. . .],
31. She uttered a curse, and unto [Apsû she spake]:
32. "What then shall we [do]?
33. "Let their way be made difficult, and let us [lie down (again) in peace]."
34. Mummu answered, and gave counsel unto Apsû,
35. [. . .] and hostile (to the gods) was the counsel Mu[mmu gave]:
36. "Come, their way is strong, but thou shalt destroy [it];
37. "Then by day shalt thou have rest, by night shalt thou lie down (in peace)."
38. Apsû [hearkened unto] him and his countenance grew bright,
39. [Since] he (i.e. Mummu) planned evil against the gods his sons.
40. [. . .] he was afraid [. . .],
41. His knees [became weak(?)], they gave way beneath him . . .

[Tablet II describes Tiamat's plot against her children, the gods, which is reported below.]

Tablet III

1. Anshar opened his mouth, and
2. [Unto Gaga], his [minister], spake the word:
3. "[O Gaga, thou minis]ter that rejoicest my spirit,
4. "[Unto Lahmu and Lah]amu will I send thee.
5. "[. . .] thou canst attain,
6. "[. . .] thou shalt cause to be brought before thee.
7. [. . . let] the gods, all of them,
8. "[Make ready for a feast], at a banquet let them sit,
9. "[Let them eat bread], let them mix wine,
10. "[That for Marduk], their avenger, they may decree the fate.
11. "[Go,] Gaga, stand before them,
12. "[And all that] I, tell thee, repeat unto them, (and say):
13. "[Anshar], your son, hath sent me,

14. "[The purpose] of his heart he hath made known unto me.
15. "[He saith that Tia]mat our mother hath conceived a hatred for us,
16. "[With all] her force she rageth, full of wrath.
17. "All the gods have turned to her,
18. "With those, whom ye created, they go at her side.
19. "They are banded together, and at the side of Tiamat they advance;
20. "They are furious, they devise mischief without resting night and day.
21. "They prepare for battle, fuming and raging;
22. "They have joined their forces and are making war.
23. "Ummu-Hubur, who formed all things,
24. "Hath made in addition weapons invincible, she hath spawned monster-serpents,
25. "Sharp of tooth and merciless of fang.
26. "With poison instead of blood she hath filled heir bodies.
27. "Fierce monster-vipers she hath clothed with terror,
28. "With splendour she hath decked them, she hath made them of lofty stature.
29. "Whoever beholdeth them, terror overcometh him,
30. "Their bodies rear up and none can withstand their attack.
31. "She hath set up vipers, and dragons, and the (monster) Lahamu,
32. "And hurricanes, and raging hounds, and scorpion-men,
33. "And mighty tempests, and fish-men, and rams;
34. They bear merciless weapons, without fear of the fight.
35. "Her commands are mighty, none can resist them;
36. "After this fashion, huge of stature, hath she made eleven (monsters).
37. "Among the gods who are her sons, inasmuch as he hath given her [support],
38. "She hath exalted Kingu; in their midst she hath raised [him] to power.
39. "To march before the forces, [to lead the host],
40. "[To] give the battle-signal, to advance [to the attack],
41. "[To direct] the battle, to control the [fight],

42. "Unto him [hath she entrusted; in costly raiment] she hath made him sit, (saying):

43. " '[I have] uttered thy spell, in the assembly of the gods [I have raised thee to power],

44. " '[The] dominion over all the gods [have I entrusted unto thee].

45. " '[Be] thou exalted, [thou] my chosen spouse,

46. " 'May they magnify thy name over all of [them . . . the Anunnaki].'

47. "She hath given him the Tablets of Destiny, on his breast she laid them, (saying):

48. " 'Thy command shall not be without avail, and the word of [thy] mouth shall be established.'

49. "Now Kingu, (thus) exalted, having received [the power of Anu],

50. "Decreed the fate for the gods, her sons, (saying):

51. " 'Let the opening of your mouth quench the Fire-god;

52. " 'Whoso is exalted in the battle, let him display (his) might!'

53. "I sent Anu, but he could not withstand her;

54. "Nudimmud was afraid and turned back.

55. "But Marduk hath set out, the director of the gods, your son;

56. "To set out against Tiamat his heart hath prompted (him).

57. "He opened his mouth and spake unto me, (saying):

58. " 'If I, your avenger,

59. " 'Conquer Tiamat and give you life,

60. " 'Appoint an assembly, make my fate preeminent and proclaim it.

61. " 'In Upshukkinaku seat yourselves joyfully together;

62. " 'With my word in place of you will I decree fate.

63. " 'May whatsoever I do remain unaltered,

64. " 'May the word of my lips never be changed nor made of no avail.'

65. "Hasten, therefore, and swiftly decree for him the fate which you bestow,

66. "That he may go and fight your strong enemy!"

67. Gaga went, he took his way and

68. Humbly before Lahmu and Lahamu, the gods, his fathers,

69. He made obeisance, and he kissed the ground at their feet.

70. He humbled himself; then he stood up and spake unto them, (saying):

[In lines 71–124, Gaga describes Tiamat's plot to the gods.]

125. Lahmu and Lahamu heard and cried aloud,

126. All of the Igigi wailed bitterly, (saying):

127. "What has been altered so that they should . . . [. . .]

128. "We do not understand the d[eed] of Tiamat!"

129. Then did they collect and go,

130. The great gods, all of them, who decree [fate].

131. They entered in before Anshar, they filled [. . .];

132. They kissed one another, in the assembly [. . .].

133. They made ready for the feast, at the banquet [they sat];

134. They ate bread, they mixed [sesame-wine].

135. The sweet drink, the mead, confused their [. . .],

136. They were drunk with drinking, their bodies were filled.

137. They were wholly at ease, their spirit was exalted;

138. Then for Marduk, their avenger, did they decree the fate.

Tablet IV

1. They prepared for him a lordly chamber,

2. Before his fathers as prince he took his place.

3. "Thou art chiefest among the great gods,

4. "Thy fate is unequalled, thy word is Anu!

5. "O Marduk, thou art chiefest among the great gods,

6. "Thy fate is unequalled, thy word is Anu!

7. "Henceforth not without avail shall be thy command,

8. "In thy power shall it be to exalt and to abase.

9. "Established shall be the word of thy mouth, irresistible shall be thy command;

10. "None among the gods shall transgress thy boundary.

11. "Abundance, the desire of the shrines of the gods,

12. "Shall be established in thy sanctuary, even though they lack (offerings).

13. "O Marduk, thou art our avenger!

14. "We give thee sovereignty over the whole world.

15. "Sit thou down in night, be exalted in thy command.

16. "Thy weapon shall never lose its power, it shall crush thy foe.

17. "O lord, spare the life of him that putteth his trust in thee,

18. "But as for the god who began the rebellion, pour out his life."

19. Then set they in their midst a garment,

20. And unto Marduk their first-born they spake:

21. "May thy fate, O lord, be supreme among the gods,

22. "To destroy and to create; speak thou the word, and (thy command) shall be fulfilled.

23. "Command now and let the garment vanish;

24. "And speak the word again and let the garment reappear!"

25. Then he spake with his mouth, and the garment vanished;

26. Again he commanded it, and the garment reappeared.

27. When the gods, his fathers, beheld (the fulfilment of) his word,

28. They rejoiced, and they did homage (unto him, saying), "Marduk is king!"

29. They bestowed upon him the sceptre, and the throne, and the ring,

30. They give him an invincible weapon, which overwhelmeth the foe.

31. "Go, and cut off the life of Tiamat,

32. "And let the wind carry her blood into secret places."

33. After the gods his fathers had decreed for the lord his fate,

34. They caused him to set out on a path of prosperity and success.

35. He made ready the bow, he chose his weapon,

36. He slung a spear upon him and fastened it . . .

37. He raised the club, in his right hand he grasped (it),

38. The bow and the quiver he hung at his side.

39. He set the lightning in front of him,

40. With burning flame he filled his body.

41. He made a net to enclose the inward parts of Tiamat,

42. The four winds he stationed so that nothing of her might escape;

43. The South wind and the North wind and the East wind and the West wind

44. He brought near to the net, the gift of his father Anu.

45. He created the evil wind, and the tempest, and the hurricane,

46. And the fourfold wind, and the sevenfold wind, and the whirlwind, and the wind which had no equal;

47. He sent forth the winds which he had created, the seven of them;

48. To disturb the inward parts of Tiamat, they followed after him.

49. Then the lord raised the thunderbolt, his mighty weapon,

50. He mounted the chariot, the storm unequalled for terror,

51. He harnessed and yoked unto it four horses,

52. Destructive, ferocious, overwhelming, and swift of pace;

53. [. . .] were their teeth, they were flecked with foam;

54. They were skilled in [. . .], they had been trained to trample underfoot.

55. [. . .], mighty in battle,

56. Left and [right . . .

57. His garment was [. . .], he was clothed with terror,

58. With overpowering brightness his head was crowned.

59. Then he set out, he took his way,

60. And toward the [rag]ing Tiamat he set his face.

61. On his lips he held [. . .],

62. . . . [. . .] he grasped in his hand.

63. Then they beheld him, the gods beheld him,

64. The gods his fathers beheld him, the gods beheld him.

65. And the lord drew nigh, he gazed upon the inward parts of Tiamat,

66. He perceived the muttering of Kingu, her spouse.

67. As (Marduk) gazed, (Kingu) was troubled in his gait,

68. His will was destroyed and his motions ceased.

69. And the gods, his helpers, who marched by his side,

70. Beheld their leader's [. . .], and their sight was troubled.

71. But Tiamat [. . .], she turned not her neck,

72. With lips that failed not she uttered rebellious words:

73. "[. . .] thy coming as lord of the gods,

74. "From their places have they gathered, in thy place are they!"

75. Then the lord [raised] the thunderbolt, his mighty weapon,

76. [And against] Tiamat, who was raging, thus he sent (the word):

77. "[Thou] art become great, thou hast exalted thyself on high,

78. "And thy [heart hath prompted] thee to call to battle.

79. "[. . .] their fathers [. . .],

80. "[. . .] their [. . .] thou hatest [. . .].

81. "[Thou hast exalted King]u to be [thy] spouse,

82. "[Thou hast . . .] him, that, even as Anu, he should issue decrees.

83. "[. . .] thou hast followed after evil,

84. "And [against] the gods my fathers thou hast contrived thy wicked plan.

85. "Let then thy host be equipped, let thy weapons be girded on!

86. "Stand! I and thou, let us join battle!"

87. When Tiamat heard these words,

88. She was like one possessed, she lost her reason.

89. Tiamat uttered wild, piercing cries,

90. She trembled and shook to her very foundations.

91. She recited an incantation, she pronounced her spell,

92. And the gods of the battle cried out for their weapons.

93. Then advanced Tiamat and Marduk, the counselor of the gods;

94. To the fight they came on, to the battle they drew nigh.

95. The lord spread out his net and caught her,

96. And the evil wind that was behind (him) he let loose in her face.

97. As Tiamat opened her mouth to its full extent,

98. He drove in the evil wind, while as yet she had not shut her lips.

99. The terrible winds filled her belly,

100. And her courage was taken from her, and her mouth she opened wide.

101. He seized the spear and burst her belly,

102. He severed her inward parts, he pierced (her) heart.

103. He overcame her and cut off her life;

104. He cast down her body and stood upon it.

105. When he had slain Tiamat, the leader,

106. Her might was broken, her host was scattered.

107. And the gods her helpers, who marched by her side,

108. Trembled, and were afraid, and turned back.

109. They took to flight to save their lives;

110. But they were surrounded, so that they could not escape.

111. He took them captive, he broke their weapons;

112. In the net they were caught and in the snare they sat down.

113. The [. . .] . . . of the world they filled with cries of grief.

114. They received punishment from him, they were held in bondage.

115. And on the eleven creatures which she had filled with the power of striking terror,

116. Upon the troop of devils, who marched at her [. . .],

117. He brought affliction, their strength [he . . .];

118. Them and their opposition he trampled under his feet.

119. Moreover, Kingu, who had been exalted over them,

120. He conquered, and with the god Dug-ga he counted him.

121. He took from him the Tablets of Destiny that were not rightly his,

122. He sealed them with a seal and in his own breast he laid them.

123. Now after the hero Marduk had conquered and cast down his enemies,

124. And had made the arrogant foe even like . . . ,

125. And had fully established Anshar's triumph over the enemy,

126. And had attained the purpose of Nudimmud,

127. Over the captive gods he strengthened his durance,

128. And unto Tiamat, whom he had conquered, he returned.

129. And the lord stood upon Tiamat's hinder parts,

130. And with his merciless club he smashed her skull.

131. He cut through the channels of her blood,

132. And he made the North wind bear it away into secret places.

133. His fathers beheld, and they rejoiced and were glad;

134. Presents and gifts they brought unto him.

135. Then the lord rested, gazing upon her dead body,

136. While he divided the flesh of the . . . , and devised a cunning plan.

137. He split her up like a flat fish into two halves;

138. One half of her he stablished as a covering for heaven.

139. He fixed a bolt, he stationed a watchman,

140. And bade them not to let her waters come forth.

141. He passed through the heavens, he surveyed the regions (thereof),

142. And over against the Deep he set the dwelling of Nudimmud.

143. And the lord measured the structure of the Deep,

144. And he founded E-shara, a mansion like unto it.

145. The mansion E-shara which he created as heaven,

146. He caused Anu, Bêl, and Ea in their districts to inhabit.

Tablet V

1. He (i.e., Marduk) made the stations for the great gods;

2. The stars, their images, as the stars of the Zodiac, he fixed.

3. He ordained the year and into sections he divided it;

4. For the twelve months he fixed three stars.

5. After he had [. . .] the days of the year [. . .] images,

6. He founded the station of Nibir to determine their bounds;

7. That none might err or go astray,

8. He set the station of Bêl and Ea along with him.

9. He opened great gates on both sides,

10. He made strong the bolt on the left and on the right.

11. In the midst thereof he fixed the zenith;

12. The Moon-god he caused to shine forth, the night he entrusted to him.

13. He appointed him, a being of the night, to determine the days;

14. Every month without ceasing with the crown he covered(?) him, (saying):

15. "At the beginning of the month, when thou shinest upon the land,

16. "Thou commandest the horns to determine six days,

17. "And on the seventh day to [divide] the crown.

18. "On the fourteenth day thou shalt stand opposite, the half [. . .].

19. "When the Sun-god on the foundation of heaven [. . .] thee,

20. "The [. . .] thou shalt cause to . . . , and thou shalt make his [. . .].

21. "[. . .] . . . unto the path of the Sun-god shalt thou cause to draw nigh,

22. "[And on the . . . day] thou shalt stand opposite, and the Sun-god shall . . . [. . .]

23. "[. . .] to traverse her way.

[The remainder of tablet V is fragmentary.]

Tablet VI

1. When Marduk heard the word of the gods,

2. His heart prompted him and he devised [a cunning plan].

3. He opened his mouth and unto Ea [he spake],

4. [That which] he had conceived in his heart he imparted [unto him]:

5. "My blood will I take and bone will I [fashion],

6. "I will make man, that man may . . . [. . .].

7. "I will create man who shall inhabit [the earth],"

8. "That the service of the gods may be established, and that [their] shrines 1 [may be built].

[The remainder of the tablet is fragmentary.]

GILGAMESH EPIC

The Gilgamesh Epic follows the adventures of (mythical?) King Gilgamesh, who reigned over Uruk. Portions of the Epic may have circulated in Sumeria as early as 2100–2000 BCE. The epic's popularity is attested by the fact that archaeologists have found fragments of it at many different sites in Mesopotamia. This tablet, which appears near the end of the epic, features Gilgamesh's friend, Utnapishtim, who tells him about how he survived the Flood.[2]

Tablet XI

1. Uta-Napishtim said unto him, to Gilgamish:
2. "I will reveal unto thee, O Gilgamish, a hidden mystery,
3. And a secret matter of the gods I will declare unto thee.
4. Shurippak, a city which thou thyself knowest,
5. On [the bank] of the river Puratti (Euphrates) is situated,
6. That city is old; and the gods [dwelling] within it
7. Their hearts induced the great gods to make a windstorm (a-bu-bi),
8. There was their father Anu,
9. Their counsellor, the warrior Enlil,
10. Their messenger En-urta [and]
11. Their prince Ennugi.
12. Nin-igi-ku, Ea, was with them [in council] and
13. reported their word to a house of reeds."

[The clamor of humanity irritated the great god Enili when it awoke him from his sleep and he decided to exterminate people. Ea learned of it and warned Uta-Napishtim in a dream.]

[FIRST SPEECH OF EA TO UTA-NAPISHTIM WHO IS SLEEPING IN A REED HUT.]

14. O House of reeds, O House of reeds! O Wall. O Wall!
15. O House of reeds, hear! O Wall, understand!
16. O man of Shurippak, son of Ubar-Tutu,
17. Throw down the house, build a ship,
18. Forsake wealth, seek after life,
19. Hate possessions, save thy life,
20. Bring all seed of life into the ship.
21. The ship which thou shalt build,
22. The dimensions thereof shall be measured,
23. The breadth and the length thereof shall be the same.
24. Then launch it upon the ocean.

[UTA-NAPISHTIM'S ANSWER TO EA.]

25. I understood and I said unto Ea, my lord:
26. See, my lord, that which thou hast ordered,
27. I regard with reverence, and will perform it,
28. But what shall I say to the town, to the multitude, and to the elders?

[SECOND SPEECH OF EA.]

29. Ea opened his mouth and spake
30. And said unto his servant, myself,
31. Thus, man, shalt thou say unto them:
32. Ill-will hath the god Enlil formed against me,
33. Therefore I can no longer dwell in your city,
34. And never more will I turn my countenance upon the soil of Enlil.
35. I will descend into the ocean to dwell with my lord Ea.
36. But upon you he will rain riches
37. A catch of birds, a catch of fish
38. . . . an [abundant] harvest,
39. . . . the sender of . . .
40. . . . shall make hail [to fall upon you].

[THE BUILDING OF THE SHIP.]

41. As soon as [something of dawn] broke . . . [Lines 49–54 broken away.]
42. The child . . . brought bitumen,
43. The strong [man] . . . brought what was needed.
44. On the fifth day I laid down its shape.
45. According to the plan its walls were 10 gar (i.e., 120 cubits) high,

[2]This text is from E.A. Wallis Budge, *The Babylonian Story of the Deluge and the Epic of Gilgamish* (1929), available at http://www.sacred-texts.com/ane/gilgdelu.htm. I have abridged the text.

46. And the width of its deck (?) was equally 10 gar.

47. I laid down the shape of its forepart and marked it out (?).

48. I covered (?) it six times.

49. ... I divided into seven,

50. Its interior I divided into nine,

51. Caulking I drove into the middle of it.

52. I provided a steering pole, and cast in all that was needful.

53. Six sar of bitumen I poured over the hull (?),

54. Three sar of pitch I poured into the inside.

55. The men who bear loads brought three sar of oil,

56. Besides a sar of oil which the tackling (?) consumed,

57. And two sar of oil which the boatman hid.

58. I slaughtered oxen for the [work] people,

59. I slew sheep every day.

60. Beer, sesame wine, oil and wine

61. I made the people drink as if they were water from the river.

62. I celebrated a feast as if it had been New Year's Day.

63. I opened [a box of ointment], I laid my hands in unguent.

64. Before the sunset (?) the ship was finished.

65. [Since] ... was difficult.

66. The shipbuilders brought the ... of the ship, above and below,

67. ... two-thirds of it.

[THE LOADING OF THE SHIP.]

68. With everything that I possessed I loaded it (i.e., the ship).

69. With everything that I possessed of silver I loaded it.

70. With everything that I possessed of gold I loaded it.

71. With all that I possessed of all the seed of life I loaded it.

72. I made to go up into the ship all my family and kinsfolk,

73. The cattle of the field, the beasts of the field, all handicraftsmen I made them go up into it.

74. The god Shamash had appointed me a time (saying)

75. The sender of . . . . . will at eventide make a hail to fall;

76. Then enter into the ship and shut thy door.

77. The appointed time drew nigh;

78. The sender of . . . . . made a hail to fall at eventide.

79. I watched the aspect of the [approaching] storm,

80. Terror possessed me to look upon it,

81. I went into the ship and shut my door.

82. To the pilot of the ship, Puzur-Enlil the sailor

83. I committed the great house (i.e., ship), together with the contents thereof.

[THE ABUBU (CYCLONE) AND ITS EFFECTS DESCRIBED.]

84. As soon as something of dawn shone in the sky

85. A black cloud from the foundation of heaven came up.

86. Inside it the god Adad thundered,

87. The gods Nabû and Sharru (i.e., Marduk) went before,

88. Marching as messengers over high land and plain,

89. Irragal (Nergal) tore out the post of the ship,

90. En-urta went on, he made the storm to descend.

91. The Anunnak brandished their torches,

92. With their glare they lighted up the land.

93. The whirlwind (or, cyclone) of Adad swept up to heaven.

94. Every gleam of light was turned into darkness.

95. . . . . . the land . . . . . as if had laid it waste.

96. A whole day long [the flood descended] ...

[1. The star-gods of the southern sky.]

97. Swiftly it mounted up . . . . . [the water] reached to the mountains

98. [The water] attacked the people like a battle.

99. Brother saw not brother.

100. Men could not be known (or, recognized) in heaven.

101. The gods were terrified at the cyclone.

102. They shrank back and went up into the heaven of Anu.

103. The gods crouched like a dog and cowered by the wall.

104. The goddess Ishtar cried out like a woman in travail.

105. The Lady of the Gods lamented with a sweet voice [saying]:

106. May that former day be turned into mud,

107. Because I commanded evil among the company of the gods.

108. How could I command evil among the company of the gods,

109. Command battle for the destruction of my people?

110. Did I of myself bring forth my people

111. That they might fill the sea like little fishes?

[UTA-NAPISHTIM'S STORY CONTINUED.]

112. The gods, the Anunnaki wailed with her.

113. The gods bowed themselves, and sat down weeping.

114. Their lips were shut tight (in distress) . . .

115. For six days and nights

116. The wind, the storm raged, and the cyclone overwhelmed the land.

[THE ABATING OF THE STORM.]

117. When the seventh day came the cyclone ceased, the storm and battle

118. which had fought like an army.

119. The sea became quiet, the grievous wind went down, the cyclone ceased.

120. I looked on the day and voices were stilled,

121. And all mankind were turned into mud,

122. The land had been laid flat like a terrace.

123. I opened the air-hole and the light fell upon my cheek,

124. I bowed myself, I sat down, I cried,

125. My tears poured down over my cheeks.

126. I looked over the quarters of the world, (to] the limits of ocean.

127. At twelve points islands appeared.

128. The ship grounded on the mountain of Nisir.

129. The mountain of Nisir held the ship, it let it not move.

130. The first day, the second day, the mountain of Nisir held the ship and let it not move.

131. The third day, the fourth day, the mountain of Nisir held the ship and let it not move.

132. The fifth day, the sixth day, the mountain of Nisir held the ship and let it not move.

133. When the seventh day had come

134. I brought out a dove and let her go free.

135. The dove flew away and [then] came back;

136. Because she had no place to alight on she came back.

137. I brought out a swallow and let her go free.

138. The swallow flew away and [then] came back;

139. Because she had no place to alight on she came back.

140. I brought out a raven and let her go free.

141. The raven flew away, she saw the sinking waters.

142. She ate, she waded (?), she rose (?), she came not back.

[UTA-NAPISHTIM LEAVES THE SHIP.]

143. Then I brought out [everything] to the four winds and made a sacrifice;

144. I set out an offering on the peak of the mountain.

145. Seven by seven I set out the vessels,

146. Under them I piled reeds, cedarwood and myrtle (?).

147. The gods smelt the savour,

148. The gods smelt the sweet savour.

149. The gods gathered together like flies over him that sacrificed.

HOMER'S *ODYSSEY*, BOOK 19, LINES 380–490

Homer's epic was written at roughly the same time as portions of the Hebrew Bible. This section of it reports Ulysses' return to his home, after wandering for 20 years. He comes *incognito* to make sure his wife, Penelope, has been loyal to him, but his plan is nearly foiled when Euryclea, the (now old) woman who had nursed him as a child, recognizes him by a scar he had received while boar hunting.[3]

Then the old woman took the cauldron in which she was going to wash his feet, and poured plenty of cold water into it, adding hot till the bath was warm enough. Ulysses sat by the fire, but ere long he turned away from the light, for it occurred to him that when the old woman had hold of his leg she would recognize a certain scar which it bore, whereon the whole truth would come out. And indeed as soon as she began washing her master, she at once knew the scar as one that had been given him by a wild boar when he was hunting on Mount Parnassus with his excellent grandfather Autolycus—who was the most accomplished thief and perjurer in the whole world—and with the sons of Autolycus. Mercury himself had endowed him with this gift, for he used to burn the thigh bones of goats and kids to him, so he took pleasure in his companionship. It happened once that Autolycus had gone to Ithaca and had found the child of his daughter just born. As soon as he had done supper Euryclea set the infant upon his knees and said, "you must find a name for your grandson; you greatly wished that you might have one."

"Son-in-law and daughter," replied Autolycus, "call the child thus: I am highly displeased with a large number of people in one place and another, both men and women; so name the child 'Ulysses,' or the child of anger. When he grows up and comes to visit his mother's family on Mount Parnassus, where my possessions lie, I will make him a present and will send him on his way rejoicing."

Ulysses, therefore, went to Parnassus to get the presents from Autolycus, who with his sons shook hands with him and gave him welcome. His grandmother Amphithea threw her arms about him, and kissed his head, and both his beautiful eyes, while Autolycus desired his sons to get dinner ready, and they did as he told them. They brought in a five year old bull, flayed it, made it ready and divided it into joints; these they then cut carefully up into smaller pieces and spitted them; they roasted them sufficiently and served the por-tions round. Thus through the livelong day to the going down of the sun they feasted, and every man had his full share so that all were satisfied; but when the sun set and it came on dark, they went to bed and enjoyed the boon of sleep.

When the child of morning, rosy-fingered Dawn, appeared, the sons of Autolycus went out with their hounds hunting, and Ulysses went too. They climbed the wooded slopes of Parnassus and soon reached its breezy upland valleys; but as the sun was beginning to beat upon the fields, fresh-risen from the slow still currents of Oceanus, they came to a mountain dell. The dogs were in front searching for the tracks of the beast they were chasing, and after them came the sons of Autolycus, among whom was Ulysses, close behind the dogs, and he had a long spear in his hand. Here was the lair of a huge boar among some thick brushwood, so dense that the wind and rain could not get through it, nor could the sun's rays pierce it, and the ground underneath lay thick with fallen leaves. The boar heard the noise of the men's feet, and the hounds baying on every side as the huntsmen came up to him, so rushed from his lair, raised the bristles on his neck, and stood at bay with fire flashing from his eyes. Ulysses was the first to raise his spear and try to drive it into the brute, but the boar was too quick for him, and charged him sideways, ripping him above the knee with a gash that tore deep though it did not reach the bone. As for the boar, Ulysses hit him on the right shoulder, and the point of the spear went right through him, so that he fell groaning in the dust until the life went out of him. The sons of Autolycus busied themselves with the carcass of the boar, and bound Ulysses' wound; then, after saying a spell to stop the bleeding, they went home as fast as they could. But when Autolycus and his sons had thoroughly healed Ulysses, they made him some splendid presents, and sent him back to Ithaca with much mutual good will. When he got back, his father and mother were rejoiced to see him, and asked him all about it, and how he had hurt himself to

---

[3]This text is from Samuel Butler's (1835–1902) translation, available at the Gutenberg project (http://promo.net/pg/index.html).

get the scar; so he told them how the boar had ripped him when he was out hunting with Autolycus and his sons on Mount Parnassus.

As soon as Euryclea had got the scarred limb in her hands and had well hold of it, she recognized it and dropped the foot at once. The leg fell into the bath, which rang out and was overturned, so that all the water was spilt on the ground; Euryclea's eyes between her joy and her grief filled with tears, and she could not speak, but she caught Ulysses by the beard and said, "My dear child, I am sure you must be Ulysses himself, only I did not know you till I had actually touched and handled you."

As she spoke she looked towards Penelope, as though wanting to tell her that her dear husband was in the house, but Penelope was unable to look in that direction and observe what was going on, for Minerva had diverted her attention; so Ulysses caught Euryclea by the throat with his right hand and with his left drew her close to him, and said, "Nurse, do you wish to be the ruin of me, you who nursed me at your own breast, now that after twenty years of wandering I am at last come to my own home again? Since it has been borne in upon you by heaven to recognize me, hold your tongue, and do not say a word about it any one else in the house, for if you do I tell you—and it shall surely be—that if heaven grants me to take the lives of these suitors, I will not spare you, though you are my own nurse, when I am killing the other women."

THE ACTS OF PAUL AND THEKLA[4]

The story of Paul's convert, Thekla, was composed during the second century, because Tertullian condemns it around 200 CE. It was probably written in the province of Asia, assembled out of oral narratives concerning Thekla. Saint Thekla was especially popular in the fourth to sixth centuries.

1. As Paul was going up to Iconium after the flight from Antioch, his fellow-travellers were Demas and Ermogenes, full of hypocrisy; and they were importunate with Paul, as if they loved him. But Paul, looking only to the goodness of Christ, did them no harm, but loved them exceedingly, so that he made the oracles of the Lord sweet to them in the teaching both of the birth and the resurrection of the Beloved; and he gave them an account, word for word, of the great things of Christ, how He had been revealed to him.

2. And a certain man, by name Onesiphorus, hearing that Paul had come to Iconium, went out to meet him with his children Silas and Zeno, and his wife Lectra, in order that he might entertain him: for Titus had informed him what Paul was like in appearance: for he had not seen him in the flesh, but only in the spirit. And he went along the road to Lystra, and stood waiting for him, and kept looking at the passers by according to the description of Titus. And he saw Paul coming, a man small in size, bald-headed, bandy-legged, well-built, with eyebrows meeting, rather long-nosed, full of grace. For sometimes he seemed like a man, and sometimes he had the countenance of an angel. And Paul, seeing Onesiphorus, smiled; and Onesiphorus said: Hail, O servant of the blessed God! And he said: Grace be with thee and thy house. And Demas and Ermogenes were jealous, and showed greater hypocrisy; so that Demas said: Are not we of the blessed God, that thou hast not thus saluted us? And Onesiphorus said: I do not see in you the fruit of righteousness; but if such you be, come you also into my house and rest yourselves.

3. And Paul having gone into the house of Onesiphorus, there was great joy, and bending of knees, and breaking of bread, and the word of God about self-control and the resurrection; Paul saying: Blessed are the pure in heart, for they shall see God: blessed are they that have kept the flesh chaste, for they shall become a temple of God: blessed are they that control themselves, for God shall speak with them: blessed are they that have kept aloof from this world, for they shall be called upright: blessed are they that have wives as not having them, for they shall receive God for their portion: blessed are they that have the fear of God, for they shall become angels of God: blessed are they that have kept the baptism, for they shall rest beside the Father and the Son: blessed are the merciful, for they shall obtain mercy, and shall not see the bitter day of judgment: blessed are the bodies of the virgins, for they shall be well pleasing to God, and shall not lose the reward of their chastity; for the word of the Father shall become to them a work of salvation against the day of His Son, and they shall have rest for ever and ever.

4. And while Paul was thus speaking in the midst of the church in the house of Onesiphorus, a certain virgin Thecla, the daughter of Theocleia, betrothed to a man named Thamyris, sitting at the window close by, listened night and day to the discourse of virginity and prayer, and did not look away from the window, but paid earnest heed to the faith, rejoicing exceedingly. And when she still saw many women going in beside Paul, she also had an eager desire to be deemed worthy to stand in the presence of Paul, and to hear the word of Christ; for never had she seen his figure, but heard his word only.

5. And as she did not stand away from the window, her mother sends to Thamyris; and he comes gladly, as if already receiving her in marriage. And Theocleia said: I have a strange story to tell thee, Thamyris; for assuredly for three days and three nights

---

[4]This text is from *Ante-Nicene Fathers,* trans. C. Coxe, vol. 8 (New York: Christian Literature Publication Company, 1885), pp. 487–492, available at http://biblestudy.churches.net/CCEL/FATHERS2/ANF08/ ANF0889.HTM#P7548_2309231. I have added paragraph numbers to facilitate study and discussion.

Thecla does not rise from the window, neither to eat nor to drink; but looking earnestly as if upon some pleasant sight, she is so devoted to a foreigner teaching deceitful and artful discourses, that I wonder how a virgin of such modesty is so painfully put about. Thamyris, this man will overturn the city of the Iconians, and thy Thecla too besides; for all the women and the young men go in beside him, being taught to fear God and to live in chastity. Moreover also my daughter, tied to the window like a spider, lays hold of what is said by Paul with a strange eagerness and awful emotion; for the virgin looks eagerly at what is said by him, and has been captivated. But do thou go near and speak to her, for she has been betrothed to thee.

6. And Thamyris going near, and kissing her, but at the same time also being afraid of her overpowering emotion, said: Thecla, my betrothed, why dost thou sit thus? and what sort of feeling holds thee overpowered? Turn round to thy Thamyris, and be ashamed. Moreover also her mother said the same things: Why dost thou sit thus looking down, my child, and answering nothing, but like a mad woman? And they wept fearfully, Thamyris indeed for the loss of a wife, and Theocleia of a child, and the maidservants of a mistress: there was accordingly much confusion in the house of mourning. And while these things were thus going on, Thecla did not turn round, but kept attending earnestly to the word of Paul.

7. And Thamyris starting up, went forth into the street, and kept watching those going in to him and coming out. And be saw two men bitterly contending with each other; and he said: Men, tell me who this is among you, leading astray the souls of young men, and deceiving virgins, so that they do not marry, but remain as they are. I promise, therefore, to give you money enough if you tell me about him; for I am the first man of the city. And Demas and Ermogenes said to him: Who this is, indeed, we do not know; but he deprives young men of wives, and maidens of husbands, saying, There is for you a resurrection in no other way, unless you remain chaste, and pollute not the flesh, but keep it chaste. And Thamyris said to them: Come into my house, and rest yourselves. And they went to a sumptuous dinner, and much wine, and great wealth, and a splendid table; and Thamyris made them drink, from his love to Thecla, and his wish to get her as his wife. And Thamyris said during the dinner: Ye men, what is his teaching, tell me, that I also may know; for I am no little distressed about Thecla, because she thus loves the stranger, and I am prevented from marrying.

8. Demas and Ermogenes said: Bring him before the governor Castelios on the charge of persuading the multitudes to embrace the new teaching of the Christians, and he will speedily destroy him, and thou shalt have Thecla as thy wife. And we shall teach thee that the resurrection of which this man speaks has taken place, because it has already taken place in the children which we have; and we rose again when we came to the knowledge of the true God.

9. And Thamyris, hearing these things, being filled with anger and rage, rising up early, went to the house of Onesiphorus with archons and public officers, and a great crowd with batons, saying: Thou hast corrupted the city of the Iconians, and her that was betrothed to me, so that she will not have me: let us go to the governor Castelios. And all the multitude said: Away with the magician; for he has corrupted all our wives, and the multitudes have been persuaded to change their opinions.

10. And Thamyris, standing before the tribunal, said with a great shout: O proconsul, this man, who he is we know not, who makes virgins averse to marriage; let him say before thee on what account he teaches these things. And Demas and Ermogenes said to Thamyris: Say that he is a Christian, and thus thou wilt do away with him. But the proconsul stayed his intention, and called Paul, saying: Who art thou, and what dost thou teach? for they bring no shall charges against thee. And Paul lifted up his voice, saying: Since I am this day examined as to what I teach, listen, O proconsul: A living God, a God of retributions, a jealous God, a God in need of nothing, consulting for the salvation of men, has sent me that I may reclaim them from corruption and uncleanness, and from all pleasure, and from death, that they may not sin. Wherefore God sent His own Son, whom I preach, and in whom I teach men to rest their hope, who alone has had compassion upon a world led astray, that they may be no lover trader judgment, O proconsul, but may have faith, and the fear of God, and the knowledge of holiness, and the

love of truth. If, therefore, I teach what has been revealed to me by God, wherein do I do wrong? And the proconsul having heard, ordered Paul to be bound, and sent to prison, until, said he, I, being at leisure, shall hear him more attentively.

11. And Thecla by night having taken off her bracelets, gave them to the gatekeeper; and the door having been opened to her, she went into the prison; and having given the jailor a silver mirror, she went in beside Paul, and, sitting at his feet, she heard the great things of God. And Paul was afraid of nothing, but ordered his life in the confidence of God. And her faith also was increased, and she kissed his bonds.

12. And when Thecla was sought for by her friends, and Thamyris, as if she had been lost, was running up and down the streets, one of the gatekeeper's fellow-slaves informed him that she had gone out by night. And having gone out, they examined the gatekeeper; and he said to them: She has gone to the foreigner into the prison. And having gone, they found her, as it were, enchained by affection. And having gone forth thence, they drew the multitudes together, and informed the governor of the circumstance. And he ordered Paul to be brought to the tribunal; but Thecla was wallowing on the ground in the place where he sat and taught her in the prison; and he ordered her too to be brought to the tribunal. And she came, exulting with joy. And the crowd, when Paul had been brought, vehemently cried out: He is a magician! away with him! But the proconsul gladly heard Paul upon the holy works of Christ. And having called a council, he summoned Thecla, and said to her: Why dost thou not obey Thamyris, according to the law of the Iconians? But she stood looking earnestly at Paul. And when she gave no answer, her mother cried out, saying: Burn the wicked wretch; burn in the midst of the theatre her that will not marry, in order that all the women that have been taught by this man may be afraid.

13. And the governor was greatly moved; and having scourged Paul, he cast him out of the city, and condemned Thecla to be burned. And immediately the governor went away to the theatre, and all the crowd went forth to the spectacle of Thecla. But as a lamb in the wilderness looks round for the shepherd, so she kept searching for Paul. And having looked upon the crowd, she saw the Lord sitting in the likeness of Paul, and said: As I am unable to endure my lot, Paul has come to see me. And she gazed upon him with great earnestness, and he went up into heaven. But the maid-servants and virgins brought the faggots, in order that Thecla might be burned. And when she came in naked, the governor wept, and wondered at the power that was in her. And the public executioners arranged the faggots for her to go up on the pile. And she, having made the sign of the cross, went up on the faggots; and they lighted them. And though a great fire was blazing, it did not touch her; for God, having compassion upon her, made an underground rumbling, and a cloud overshadowed them from above, full of water and hail; and all that was in the cavity of it was poured out, so that many were in danger of death. And the fire was put out, and Thecla saved.

14. And Paul was fasting with Onesiphorus and his wife, and his children, in a new tomb, as they were going from Iconium to Daphne. And when many clays were past, the fasting children said to Paul: We are hungry, and we cannot buy loaves; for Onesiphorus had left the things of the world, and followed Paul, with all his house. And Paul, having taken off his cloak, said: Go, my child, buy more loaves, and bring them. And when the child was buying, he saw Thecla their neighbour, and was astonished, and said: Thecla, whither art thou going? And she said: I have been saved from the fire, and am following Paul. And the boy said: Come, I shall take thee to him; for he is distressed about thee, and is praying six days. And she stood beside the tomb where Paul was with bended knees, and praying, and saying: O Saviour Christ, let not the fire touch Thecla, but stand by her, for she is Thine. And she, standing behind him, cried out: O Father, who hast made the heaven and the earth, the Father of Thy holy Son, I bless Thee that Thou hast saved me that I may see Paul. And Paul, rising up, saw her, and said: O God, that knowest the heart, the Father of our Lord Jesus Christ, I bless Thee that Thou, having heard me, hast done quickly what I wished.

15. And they had five loaves, and herbs, and water; and they rejoiced in the holy works of Christ. And Thecla said to Paul: I shall cut

my hair, and follow thee whithersoever thou mayst go. And he said: It is a shameless age, and thou art beautiful. I am afraid lest another temptation come upon thee worse than the first, and that thou withstand it not, but be cowardly. And Thecla said: Only give me the seal in Christ, and temptation shall not touch me. And Paul said: Thecla, wait with patience, and thou shalt receive the water.

16. And Paul sent away Onesiphorus and all his house to Iconium; and thus, having taken Thecla, he went into Antioch. And as they were going in, a certain Syriarch, Alexander by name, seeing Thecla, became enamoured of her, and tried to gain over Paul by gifts and presents. But Paul said: I know not the woman whom thou speakest of, nor is she mine. But he, being of great power, himself embraced her in the street. But she would not endure it, but looked about for Paul. And she cried out bitterly, saying: Do not force the stranger; do not force the servant of God. I am one of the chief persons of the Iconians; and because I would not have Thamyris, I have been cast out of the city. And taking hold of Alexander, she tore his cloak, and pulled off his crown, and made him a laughing-stock. And he, at the same time loving her, and at the same time ashamed of what had happened, led her before the governor; and when she had confessed that she had done these things, he condemned her to the wild beasts. And the women were struck with astonishment, and cried out beside the tribunal: Evil judgment! impious judgment! And she asked the governor, that, said she, I may remain pure until I shall fight with the wild beasts. And a certain Tryphaena, whose daughter was dead, took her into keeping, and had her for a consolation.

17. And when the beasts were exhibited, they bound her to a fierce lioness; and Tryphaena accompanied her. But the lioness, with Thecla sitting upon her, licked her feet; and all the multitude was astonished. And the charge on her inscription was: Sacrilegious. And the women cried out from above: An impious sentence has been passed in this city! And after the exhibition, Tryphaena again receives her. For her daughter Falconilla had died, and said to her in a dream: Mother, thou shalt have this stranger Thecla in my place, in order that she may pray concerning me, and that I may be transferred to the place of the just.

18. And when, after the exhibition, Tryphaena received her, at the same time indeed she grieved that she had to fight with the wild beasts on the day following; and at the same time, loving her as much as her daughter Falconilla, she said: My, second child Thecla, come and pray for my child, that she may live for ever; for this I saw in my sleep. And she, nothing hesitating, lifted up her voice, and said: God most high, grant to this woman according to her wish, that her daughter Falconilla may live for ever. And when Thecla had thus spoken, Tryphaena lamented, considering so much beauty thrown to the wild beasts.

19. And when it was dawn, Alexander came to take her, for it was he that gave the hunt, saying: The governor is sitting, and the crowd is in uproar against us. Allow me to take away her that is to fight with the wild beasts. And Tryphaena cried aloud, so that he even fled, saying: A second mourning for my Falconilla has come upon my house and there is no one to help; neither child, for she is dead, nor kinsman, for I am a widow. God of Thecla, help her!

20. And immediately the governor sends an order that Thecla should be brought. And Tryphaena, taking her by the hand, said: My daughter Falconilla, indeed, I took away to the tomb; and thee, Thecla, I am taking to the wild-beast fight. And Thecla wept bitterly, saying: O Lord, the God in whom I believe, to whom I have fled for refuge, who deliveredst me from the fire, do Thou grant a recompense to Tryphaena, who has had compassion on Thy servant, and because she has kept me pure. Then a tumult arose, and a cry of the people, and the women sitting together, the one saying: Away with the sacrilegious person! the others saying: Let the city be raised against this wickedness. Take off all of us, O proconsul! Cruel sight! evil sentence!

21. And Thecla, having been taken out of the hand of Tryphaena, was stripped, and received a girdle, and was thrown into the arena, and lions and bears and a fierce lioness were let loose upon her; and the lioness having run up to her feet, lay down; and the multitude of the women cried aloud. And a bear ran upon her; but the lioness, meeting the bear, tore her to pieces. And again a lion that had been trained against men, which belonged to Alexander, ran upon

her; and she, the lioness, encountering the lion, was killed along with him. And the women made great lamentation, since also the lioness, her protector, was dead.

22. Then they sent in many wild beasts, she standing and stretching forth her hands, and praying. And when she had finished her prayer, she turned and saw a ditch full of water, and said: Now it is time to wash myself. And she threw herself in, saying: In the name of Jesus Christ I am baptized on my last day. And the women seeing, and the multitude, wept, saying: Do not throw thyself into the water; so that also the governor shed tears, because the seals were going to devour such beauty. She then threw herself in the name of Jesus Christ; but the seals having seen the glare of the fire of lightning, floated about dead. And there was round her, as she was naked, a cloud of fire; so that neither could the wild beasts touch her, nor could she be seen naked.

23. And the women, when other wild beasts were being thrown in, wailed. And some threw sweet-smelling herbs, others nard, others cassia, others amomum, so that there was abundance of perfumes. And all the wild beasts that had been thrown in, as if they had been withheld by sleep, did not touch her; so that Alexander said to the governor: I have bulls exceedingly terrible; let us bind to them her that is to fight with the beasts. And the governor, looking gloomy, turned, and said: Do what thou wilt. And they bound her by the feet between them, and put red-hot irons under the privy parts of the bulls, so that they, being rendered more furious, might kill her. They rushed about, therefore; but the burning flame consumed the ropes, and she was as if she had not been bound. But Tryphaena fainted standing beside the arena, so that the crowd said: Queen Tryphaena is dead. And the governor put a stop to the games, and the city was in dismay. And Alexander entreated the governor, saying: Have mercy both on me and the city, and release this woman. For if Caesar hear of these things, he will speedily destroy the city also along with us, because his kinswoman Queen Tryphaena has died beside the Abaci.

24. And the governor summoned Thecla out of the midst of the wild beasts, and said to her: Who art thou? and what is there about thee, that not one of the wild beasts touches thee?

And she said: I indeed am a servant of the living God; and as to what there is about me, I have believed in the Son of God, in whom He is well pleased; wherefore not one of the beasts has touched me. For He alone is the end of salvation, and the basis of immortal life; for He is a refuge to the tempest-tossed, a solace to the afflicted, a shelter to the despairing; and, once for all, whoever shall not believe on Him, shall not live for ever.

25. And the governor having heard this, ordered her garments to be brought, and to be put on. And Thecla said: He that clothed me naked among the wild beasts, will in the day of judgment clothe thee with salvation. And taking the garments, she put them on. The governor therefore immediately issued an edict, saying: I release to you the God-fearing Thecla, the servant of God. And the women shouted aloud, and with one mouth returned thanks to God, saying: There is one God, the God of Thecla; so that the foundations of the theatre were shaken by their voice. And Tryphaena having received the good news, went to meet the holy Thecla, and said: Now I believe that the dead are raised: now I believe that my child lives. Come within, and I shall assign to thee all that is mine. She therefore went in along with her, and rested eight days, having instructed her in the word of God, so that most even of the maid-servants believed. And there was great joy in the house.

26. And Thecla kept seeking Paul; and it was told her that he was in Myra of Lycia. And taking young men and maidens, she girded herself; and having sewed the tunic so as to make a man's cloak, she came to Myra, and found Paul speaking the word of God. And Paul was astonished at seeing her, and the crowd with her, thinking that some new trial was coming upon her. And when she saw him, she said: I have received the baptism, Paul; for He that wrought along with thee for the Gospel has wrought in me also for baptism. And Paul, taking her, led her to the house of Hermaeus, and hears everything from her, so that those that heard greatly wondered, and were comforted, and prayed over Tryphaena. And she rose up, and said: I am going to Iconium. And Paul said: Go, and teach the word of God. And Tryphaena sent her much clothing and gold, so that she left to Paul many things for the service of the poor.

27. And she went to Iconium. And she goes into the house of Onesiphorus, and fell upon the pavement where Paul used to sit and teach her, and wept, saying: God of myself and of this house, where Thou didst make the light to shine upon me, O Christ Jesus, the Son of the living God, my help in the fire, my help among the wild beasts, Thou art glorified for ever. Amen. And she found Thamyris dead, but her mother alive. And having sent for her mother, she said: Theocleia, my mother, canst thou believe that the Lord liveth in the heavens? For whether thou desirest wealth, God gives it to thee through me; or thy child, I am standing beside thee. And having thus testified, she departed to Seleucia, and dwelt in a cave seventy-two years, living upon herbs and water. And she enlightened many by the word of God.

28. And certain men of the city, being Greeks by religion, and physicians by profession, sent to her insolent young men to destroy her. For they said: She is a virgin, and serves Artemis, and from this she has virtue in healing. And by the providence of God she entered into the rock alive, and went under ground. And she departed to Rome to see Paul, and found that he had fallen asleep. And after staying there no long time, she rested in a glorious sleep; and she is buried about two or three stadia from the tomb of her master Paul.

29. She was cast, then, into the fire when seventeen years old, and among the wild beasts when eighteen. And she was an ascetic in the cave, as has been said, seventy-two years, so that all the years of her life were ninety. And having accomplished many cures, she rests in the place of the saints, having fallen asleep on the twenty-fourth of the month of September in Christ Jesus our Lord, to whom be glory and strength for ever and ever. Amen.